CRISIS AND CONTENTION IN SOCIOLOGY

CRISIS AND CONTENTION IN SOCIOLOGY

Edited by

TOM BOTTOMORE

SAGE Studies in International Sociology 1
sponsored by the International Sociological Association/ISA

For information address

SAGE Publications Ltd.
44 Hatton Garden
London EC 1

SAGE Publications Inc.
275 South Beverly Drive
Beverly Hills, California 90012

International Standard Book Number
0 8039 9955 0 Cloth
0 8039 9962 3 Paper

Library of Congress Catalog Card Number
75-24787

First Printing

Printed in Great Britain by
Biddles Ltd., Guildford, Surrey.

CONTENTS

PREFACE

Tom Bottomore
University of Sussex

The essays brought together in this volume are revised versions of papers which were originally written for a round table meeting at the 8th World Congress of Sociology, held in Toronto in August 1974. Regrettably, three of the authors – Igor Kon, Ivan Kuvačić and A. K. Saran – were unable to attend the Congress, and their contributions to the discussion were greatly missed. I am grateful to them for having agreed to the publication of their papers, and for the trouble they have taken in revising them.

At the Congress itself there was a lively debate, which took place in two stages. First, the four contributors who were present (and Yuri Zamoshkin whom we invited to join the panel) conducted, under my chairmanship, a public seminar discussion, starting from the issues raised by Franco Ferrarotti in his introductory paper. This was followed by a broader discussion in which members of the audience participated, posing questions to the authors of the papers and raising additional points of their own. It would be impossible in this short preface to convey, in any adequate way, the whole substance of this wide-ranging debate, and I shall confine myself to commenting on what seemed to be the salient themes.

In the first place, it should be noted that while the notion of an existing 'crisis' in sociology was generally accepted, there was considerable disagreement about its extent, its novelty, and its significance. As Franco Ferrarotti points out, sociology was born from a major social and cultural crisis, and its development has been, in large measure, a response to new crises; to the transformations brought about by industrial development, by wars and revolutions. The intellectual crises *within* sociology are one aspect of these more general conditions, for sociology, like all the human sciences, is a part of the general culture and subject to all the influences that arise from the clash of interests and the diversity of cultural orientations. From the beginning, there have been divergent viewpoints in sociology – competing theories and conceptual schemes – so that it could be characterized, in the words of Margaret Masterman, as a science with 'too many paradigms'.[1] Nevertheless, there have been occasions when something like a paradigm change has occurred, not in the relatively clear-cut fashion that may prevail in some other sciences, but at least in the sense of a movement from one broad array of concepts and categories to a different one, within which there is still, however, a considerable diversity of specific approaches and theories. We could perhaps describe this as a movement from one 'quasi-paradigm' to another.

Something of the kind seems to have taken place at the end of the nineteenth century, in what Stuart Hughes has singled out as a major 'reorientation of European social thought',[2] which had two principal elements: a critique of Marxism and a revolt against positivism. But this reorientation was far from complete or definitive. Marxism, as a social theory, not only survived but flourished in the early decades of the twentieth century, in the works of the Austro-Marxists, of Karl Korsch, Lukács, Gramsci, and the Frankfurt School. Similarly, positivism, in a broad sense, acquired a stronger influence in sociology as a whole, as well as in some versions of Marxism. So much so, that one of the main themes of critical self-reflection in the 1960s and 1970s is once again the inadequacy, or the invalidity, of positivism in the social sciences. The situation which prevailed from 1945 to the end of the 1950s, in which a single paradigm – structural-functionalism – appeared to be pre-eminent, was perhaps an unusual one; and in any event there were alternative paradigms, such as Marxism, which were overshadowed only in certain spheres of academic sociology.

It may still be asked, though, whether the present crisis is not more profound, more fundamental, than those which preceded it; whether we are not at a turning point such as Max Weber described, when '. . . men become uncertain about the significance of the viewpoints which they have used unreflectively . . . the path becomes lost in the dusk . . . [and] science also prepares to change its standpoint and its conceptual apparatus in order to look down from the heights of thought upon the current of events'. There are two separate questions here, which need to be carefully distinguished. Is there, first, a cultural crisis, a rapid and thoroughgoing 'transvaluation of all values', one source of which may be found, at least in the industrial societies (as many recent social thinkers have claimed) in the recognition of limits to economic growth, of limited resources, and of the fragility of the balance between human society and nature, exemplified most strikingly by the ever-present threat of nuclear disaster; and is the confusion that reigns in sociological thought itself simply a manifestation of this crisis? Or is it rather that sociology, as an autonomous intellectual discipline, is experiencing its present difficulties only because it has not yet succeeded in adapting its conceptual apparatus to the rapid flux of events and the emergence of new problems? I think we must take account of both features: sociology is in some degree autonomous and objective, and as a body of systematic thought it is going through a period of radical reorientation of its theoretical interests and models, in the course of which there is bound to be diversity, contention and uncertainty; but at the same time, sociology can never wholly escape the influence of the whole culture in which it is embedded and which shapes in manifold ways its background assumptions and preoccupations.

Hence we might say that there are two (related) crises: a very general cultural crisis, and an intellectual or theoretical crisis in the particular sphere of sociological thought. But there is a further complication. The following essays make evident, as did the round table discussion, that the idea of a crisis – in both the broader and narrower sense – is given quite a different meaning by sociologists living in diverse cultural situations and under different political regimes. Amando de Miguel, for example, refers to the 'critical conditions' in which sociologists have to work, particularly in authoritarian countries, where their desire to study important social phenomena is often frustrated by the opposition of ruling groups and entrenched orthodoxies. In such societies it is mainly a question of being able to develop sociological research at all, and to establish sociology as an academic discipline in the face of a traditional literary and philosophical culture, or of political hostility.

From an entirely different standpoint A. K. Saran also discusses one aspect of this question; namely, the relation between sociology and traditional thought. In his view, the crisis in sociology springs from its failure to achieve (and its inherent incapacity to achieve) its original goal of establishing a 'new universalism' that would replace the universalism of the forsaken traditional theology and metaphysics. In a different terminology, which also expresses the presuppositions of another paradigm, Igor Kon and Ivan Kuvacić refer to a similar feature of the crisis (in a more restricted sphere) which they identify as the inability of sociology to support any longer the social integration of Western capitalist society. Kuvacić indeed goes farther, and suggests that if Marxism assumes the role of upholding the integration of existing society in the socialist countries it will experience (has perhaps already begun to experience) the same kind of crisis. By contrast, he emphasizes what he regards, historically, as the critical function of sociology, and describes its 'authentic form' as a *comparative-critical reflection* upon society.

Thus one way of confronting the crisis is to argue that sociology should develop as a *critical* rather than a *positive* science. But this poses the problem of the universal presuppositions that would constitute the ground of any systematic critical reflection, and so appears to drive us back to the need for a philosophy of history or a philosophy of human nature. Norman Birnbaum's essay raises the possibility of an end of sociology as a separate discipline, and seems to suggest that its broader interests in interpreting the development of societies might find a place within a 'philosophical anthropology' which would draw very widely upon the work of other human sciences – among them economics, history and psychoanalysis.

Another response, which is intimated in Ferrarotti's essay, and discussed in some detail by Stefan Nowak, is to say that sociology should renounce its more grandiose ambitions, and while not abandoning its claim to be a *theoretical* science, should concentrate upon the cumulative development of empirically tested propositions and theories, even within a very limited range of phenomena. In this way, Nowak argues, sociology might make a greater contribution than it does at present to guiding social action; though it would still be necessary to take into account, in a more general way, the relations between sociology and society, and the possible instrumental and ideological functions of sociology, in order to minimize the abuse of its findings.

Nowak's essay touches upon another issue which assumed some importance in the debate, and is mentioned specifically by other contributors. The idea of a 'crisis' in sociology does not imply at all that there is a 'depression'. On the contrary, we have been living through a period of 'boom', in which there has been a vast growth of sociological teaching and research, not only in those countries where the subject was already well-established but in other parts of the world as well. Hence, even in a situation where there are 'too many paradigms', and a confused confrontation takes place between armies grappling in the night, research findings and ideas emerge from within each paradigm and demonstrate a limited usefulness in two ways: they increase and diffuse knowledge of social life (at the lowest, in a descriptive way), and they are 'applied' to social policy, not only in a technological sense but also politically. I do not think there can be any doubt that sociology, in many countries, does now influence, for good or ill, the policies that are adopted and the manner in which they are executed, in education, public administration, and a wide range of social services. As Nowak says, we should try to ensure that the influence is for good – and that is a complex matter. It would be foolish to ignore these practical issues, and the empirical research that bears directly upon them, only because we do not have a satisfactory global interpretation of man and society.

The divergent interpretations of the 'crisis' obviously arise from differences in the commitment of individual thinkers to particular theoretical systems or conceptions of the nature of a social science, as well as from the diversity of cultural and political contexts in which they produce their ideas. Nevertheless, it seems to me exceptionally important to recognize the impact upon sociology at the present time of the increasing contact between different types of society and different civilizations, which has begun to undermine that predominance of 'Western' social science which several contributors to this volume criticize, and has led to a very intense debate about the 'universality' or 'parochialism' of sociological concepts, and about the problems of understanding 'alien cultures'. It would be impossible now to examine adequately the changes in sociological thinking in terms of a reorientation merely of European, or even Western, social thought. The emergence onto the historical scene of nations that previously lived in obscurity, or were described and interpreted mainly from the outside (from the perspective of other nations who fitted them into *their* conception of the world) has evidently provoked a profound reassessment of sociological ideas; and it is this real and complex transformation of the world that largely explains the contentious, confused and uncertain character of sociology today. But it is at least one of the virtues of sociology that it constitutes an intellectual arena in which the major problems of a world in transition can be formulated and systematically examined, and even, as the more optimistic (or more naive) among us may be inclined to think, eventually be more fully understood and more effectively attacked.

NOTES

[1] Margaret Masterman, 'The Nature of a Paradigm', in *Criticism and the Growth of Knowledge*, ed. I. Lakatos and A. Musgrave (Cambridge: Cambridge University Press, 1970), 58-59.

[2] H. Stuart Hughes, *Consciousness and Society* (New York: Oxford University Press, 1958).

1

INTRODUCTORY COMMENTS ON THE THEME:
Is There a Crisis in Sociology?

Franco Ferrarotti
Institute of Sociology, University of Rome

I am well aware that the question, while in itself legitimate, sounds largely superfluous. Sociology was born out of a major historical crisis. Crises have accompanied and stimulated its development. Far from being inhibited, sociology thrives on them. Crisis is nothing new to sociology. Its official founder, Auguste Comte, could not conceive of any other relevant function for sociology except the reorganization of society based on a scientific clarification of ideas to be used as cornerstones in the building up of social consensus. Rather than the 'science of society', sociology should perhaps more appropriately be called the 'science of social crisis'.

What seems peculiar to the present day intellectual scene, however, is that the crisis does not concern only a given society to be analyzed and reorganized according to rational criteria with the decisive help of sociology. At the present time, the crisis seems to have entered into the very substance of sociology itself, both as a specific field of learning and as an instrument for social experimenting. There again, one should not forget that sociology has gone through other critical and difficult phases in its two-century old evolution.

Already by the second half of the nineteenth century, it became apparent that the high ambitions of the official founder, who would see sociology as the *scientia scientiarum* as well as the operational tool for the rational transformation of society, not to mention the aims and theories of Marx, Proudhon, and others, were by and large misplaced ambitions, at least insofar as these thinkers believed it possible to set definite goals and outcomes of historical development through the discovery of social laws quite similar to a natural law. It is true that these early sociologists, whom I would describe as systematic because they appear to be concerned with society as a global, rational, and therefore, fully intelligible structure, or tendentially closed system, never look as if they had doubts about the future of human society. They talk to humanity in the name of humanity. For them, there is no division of scientific labour yet. They criticize existing conditions but they never seem to have lost their front-door key, as it were. They write about alienation, but they seem to know exactly where we come from, where we are now, and where we are bound to go. Great outsiders, their style of work is that of the classical craftsman: independent, autonomous, individualistic.

The systematic season did not last very long. Sociology soon became one academic discipline among others. Its object of study ceased to be mankind or history as such. Despite the extraordinary insight by the young Marx (in the *Manuscripts of 1844*) that 'there will be only one science', including natural and social sciences, sociology tended to be more analytically defined and specialized. Before the century was over, Durkheim had severely criticized his great predecessors, Comte and Spencer, on account of their generalaties. But was the academic community, in its structures and personnel, ready to accept sociology in the full sense: that is to say a science which is also a consciousness; a detached scientific analysis which is, at the same time, necessarily a social intervention; an objective research in which, however, observer and observed tend, in the last instance, to coincide, making personal involvement inescapable?

The fact can be distasteful to many professional sociologists, understandably eager to become or to remain respectable members of the scientific community, but it should nevertheless be recognized and flatly stated there is a basic ambiguity in the sociological enterprise which comes from far back. It is connected with its very beginning and it carries to this day a considerable weight in the present crisis. It should always be kept in mind as it cannot be dispelled by any trick. Too many descriptions of the crisis in sociology take the crisis for granted as a uniquely sociological phenomenon and are more psychological than intellectual. They reveal a disappointment which probably comes from excessive expectation. No matter how verbally daring and iconoclastic these descriptions are, in fact, if carefully analyzed, they show a fairly awkward rationalization of individual troubles or personal positions. They usually boil down to outright self-justification. They are perhaps linked also with an uncritical idealization of science in general and should be regarded as a kind of intellectual hangover, the importance of which, as a symptom, is not to be minimized. Whoever was, until recently, ready to rely completely, or I should perhaps say religiously, on quantitative methods or on mathematical models applied to social phenomena, to the point of risking the quantification of the qualitative, is now likely to repent so sweepingly as to swing to the extreme opposite position of renouncing any theoretical and logically grounded approach in favour of an immediate and total immersion in praxis. It is prima facie evident that the same idealizing or para-mystical attitude is here at work. Substituting Carnap or Lazarsfeld with Mao is hardly a way out of present difficulties.

This state of things should not justify any self-complacent irony on the part of self-styled 'esprits forts'. If there is a crisis in sociology at the present time, it is only natural that its first dimension should be the one which concerns directly the person of the sociologist, his self-image as a professional and his basic commitment as a citizen. After all, it is through individual sociologists that sociology lives and expresses itself in the world.

The danger lies in the reductionist tendency to view such a crisis simply as the outcome of some sort of personal maladjustment. There is some truth in this, to be sure, but it would be grossly misleading to confine the sociological malaise to its personal or psychological components. It should, in the first place, be noticed that this uncomfortable feeling of inadequacy, of not being quite up to the challenge of the times, and actually of being taken by surprise, if not altogether mastered, by events, of not being free from economic and social constraints, is not confined to sociology but concerns science and scientific activity in its wider meaning, especially as regards its implications. The crisis in sociology is not, therefore, an exclusively sociological matter. The idea of science as a smooth, self-correcting flow of cumulative knowledge, providing new theories as soon as new facts emerge which would not be explicable in terms of the old established theories, has been proven to be untenable.

There is a growing awareness that science can no longer be regarded as a secular religion, as a viable substitute for old-time dogmatic certainties. It is only a human enterprise, exposed to the risk of regression, whose history is full of economic pressure, power struggles, and mental and physical persecution. The second dimension of the crisis in sociology recalls, it seems, a more global crisis, a science crisis, concerning its place in the history of mankind, its final meaning and its social function. One used to think in terms of pure science and applied science. One used to question the technical viability and eventually the ethical acceptability of the application of scientific results to the production process. But the distinction between pure science and applied science is now clearly obsolete. Science is no longer connected with production through a technical mediation. It has been incorporated into the production process; it has become a direct productive force.

Under present day circumstances, the problem is rather a problem of control: science for whom and for what, and, first of all, science in whose interest? We had forgotten about economic interests as far as science is concerned. The scientific revolution appeared as a neutral enterprise, far above any trivial, petty economic worry, a superior task. Scientists themselves were regarded as the new apostles for a new humanity: rational, unselfish, basically just, naturally democratic. These obvious corollaries of a technocratic mentality incapable of grasping the human meaning of science have found their inspired expression in the famous booklet by C. P. Snow (*The Two Cultures and the Scientific Revolution*).

Sociology in crisis is then part and parcel of science in crisis. The sociologist is in quest of a new self-image, as much as is the nuclear physicist, or the historian or the economist. The terms of such quest are obviously different. But this difference has little to do with anguished introspectiveness or internal dispositions; it depends essentially on the needs of the society as they are expressed by the various publics corresponding to the various and contrasting social strata and classes of which society is composed. Now, to what public do sociologists address themselves today? No clear-cut answer seems, for the time being, satisfactory. But this is certainly the third major dimension of the crisis. To whom are sociologists talking today? We have seen that systematic sociologists used to talk and write for humanity as a whole. At present, however, sociologists prefer to talk and write for specialized publics – any general sociological contribution would rather fall in the domain of social philosophy and would not seem to be able to meet the essential scientific requirements for serious professional recognition. The fact is that the bulk of practising sociologists today address themselves to academic colleagues. Even though later and to a lesser degree than other more ancient disciplines, sociology has become, more or less everywhere, institutionalized. Institutionalization is both a protection and a barrier. It tends to separate the sociologist from his specific society and from the peculiar needs of his immediate social environment. He then tends to view these needs as contingent problems. At worst, he might simply forget that sociology is not the object of sociology.

The third dimension of the sociology crisis seems, therefore, to be twofold. On one hand, there are the problems posed by a process of institutionalization within the framework of traditional academic structures which were historically formed and developed long before sociology emerged as a relatively autonomous field of scholarship. On the other hand, one must take into account the demands made by society upon sociology in terms of social intervention and social engineering, almost as if sociology were a magic art. Moreover, one should not overlook the frustrating effect that many of these requests have upon sociologists whenever a purely instrumental character, attributed to research and its findings, is transparent.

In this connection, the terms of a fourth dimension of the crisis become fairly clear. This dimension is no longer psychological nor organizational nor purely institutional. It is substantive and strikes at the very heart of the discipline. It has to do with the construction of the conceptual frameworks whereby the gathering of empirical data is coherently and significantly guided. Especially under the important influence of Talcott Parsons, contemporary sociology has made an extreme effort towards abstracting a concept of society as a system at such a high level that the historical bases and characteristics of social phenomena have been practically obliterated. This has permitted a certain degree of formal reasoning but at the price of being unable to describe and eventually explain relevant issues in a specific historical situation. The historical, dynamic nature of sociological concepts has been overlooked in the hope of building a universal body, timeless and spaceless, of sociological theory. That such effort would bring about mechanical transfers of concepts from one historical and economic context to another and that, even more seriously, as David Lockwood and others have soon pointed out, would lead social research to a static meta-historical Utopia are nothing to be startled by. They are only the necessary consequences once the historical dialectical nature of sociological concepts has been denied or misunderstood. In this sense, the importance of Talcott Parsons' work can hardly be overrated, and does not seem to depend only on the fact that for many years Professor Parsons was the pre-eminent sociologist at Harvard. It also depends strictly on intellectual factors stemming from the centrality, or crucial quality, of his intention, which has been quite clear since *The Structure of Social Action* (1937). It consists in the elaboration of the concept of society as a system at a level of abstraction sufficiently high to permit subsuming under it, as subsystems, at least the concept of culture and the concept of personality. The framework made up by social structure, culture, and personality is the threefold grid which, according to Parsons, would enable sociology to cope with any relevant social phenomenon irrespective of historical background or economic way of production or ideological orientation. In this way, Parsons' sociology presents itself as the final and highest stage of sociological thinking, while representing, both domestically and from the point of view of international relations, a refined rationalization of the strategic needs of the American system (unifying coherence internally and instrumental hegemonic activism abroad); and, in this respect, the two volumes of *Theories of Society* are quite revealing. This kind of sociology, perhaps the most sophisticated version of official, or academically accepted, sociology, is certainly in crisis today, confronted as we are with large-scale events in the United States and in the world which seem difficult or impossible to accommodate within that framework and which, on the basis of that conceptual scheme, there was apparently no way of predicting.

These considerations could be helpful not so much in deciding whether there is or is not a crisis in sociology, but rather in establishing what kind of crisis and what is to be done about it. Far too many explanations of the crisis have a purely *internal* character; they tend to explain and limit the crisis of sociology in terms of a technical breakdown, or of a failure to realize the political relevance of social research, or of a lack of financial autonomy. But they don't seem to recognize, in its full import, the fact that the problems of sociology as a discipline are closely connected with the practical (objective) issues confronting the larger society, the mechanisms and the institutions which regulate its functioning. In this perspective, no catastrophic or romantic meaning should be attached to the word crisis. Crisis is distressing and painful but also revealing, epiphanic. As far as sociology is concerned, it is a crisis of growth, not of exhaustion. And the present state of crisis, if seen in its proper light, that is, not as an exclusively personal trouble, becomes important in order to rediscover and to reassert the nature of the sociological enterprise, its necessarily unfinished character, its problematic disposition, its ambiguity. It could also open our eyes to what 'being a sociologist' means, that is to say to the importance of 'being a man among men' and to the advisability, in order to recapture its original meaning beyond any illusion of ethical neutrality, of passing from 'sociology as separation' to 'sociology as participation'.

Basic questions remain unanswered. In the first place, if it is true that definite value orientations and political presuppositions are implicit in any social research, should then the sociologist be purely and simply equated with the day-to-day politician or policy maker? Most radical sociologists would answer in the affirmative and would, therefore, be trapped by the contradiction between political immediatism and the scientific mediation of political relevance. They would be finished as sociologists without being sure of their rebirth as politicians.

In the second place, if it is true that sociology is connected with its specific historical and economic background, then there will be a plurality of sociologies or schools. Are these various sociological schools (corresponding to different value orientations and to different objective backgrounds) bound to:

(a) ignore one another;

(b) dogmatically fight one another;

(c) or is it possible, and desirable, to have an intellectual exchange among them?

In the end, having rediscovered sociology as a *science in permanent tension,* the phrase 'sociology in crisis' and its ready-made prescriptions lose much of their appeal.

In particular, their limitations become apparent in the perennial fluctuation from an internal critique of the Parsonian evolutionary universals and the necessity of a clear denunciation of their ideological nature. A most urgent task, in this connection, seems to me the rediscovery of the importance of Marxism for sociology and the recapturing, as it were, of its sociological soul. I know, of course, that there are many Marxisms, just as, with one Christ, there are many Christian religions. What seems important is not to confine ourselves to the official Soviet version of Marxism, no matter how tempting the symmetrical parallel with the Parsonian systematic sociology in the end might be. What should be called into question is the way in which social theory is being built. It would be, in my opinion, a sad mistake to think that only formalistic theories developed within academic institutions are worth considering as scientifically relevant. Marxism after Marx offers us quite an example of a theory of great scientific and political relevance that has been developed outside, if not against, academia. Let's face it, if Weber and the Weberians, Parsons and the functionalists, old and new, have constantly reacted to Marxism, this has happened not on the basis of scientific premises or of technical developments of the theoretical framework, but rather under the pressure of real, practical conflicts, both economic and political, which would radically question the institutional fabric underlying the legitimation of their theory. The construction of social theory should not be confused with an abstract model building, essentially meta-historical and apolitical and in the end, at best, tautological. We should learn from Marx and practise the 'rule of historically determined abstraction'. It implies a constant back and forth between the theoretical level, field work and political, practical involvement in such a way as to give rise to a process of mutual fertilization and enrichment between theory and practice.

Some fifteen years ago, I published, in Italian, a book called *Sociology as Participation.* The book is now out of print; it was not quite understood, and I mean this literally. Nobody can understand Italian nowadays. Not even opera singers. The book fell flat between the autobiographical lamentations of a dissatisfied, part-time politician, and the do-goodness of a half-baked Marxist social worker. *Habent sua fata libelli.* What I wanted to convey, however, was that we need a radical reorientation: from science as separation to science as participation, practical involvement, political commitment; a return to science as a human, all too human enterprise. I don't think involvement is a moral or, worse, a philanthropic exigency; it is a cognitive, scientific requirement. Nor do I think that passing from Parsonian functionalism to ethnomethodology would be a way out. Undoubtedly, sociological analysis is inevitably dependent on the common-sense understandings sociologists have as members of the society they are studying. The implication drawn by the ethnomethodologists is that these common-sense understandings must not be used as an unexamined resource as in conventional sociology but must be made a topic of enquiry. In this way, they try to mark out a domain which is distinct from the concerns of the actors themselves; for instance, which would treat talk as a topic rather than a resource – a domain taken for granted by actors, or members. Thus, the ethnomethodologists seek to re-establish the scientificity of sociology and avoid the crisis of not being able to distinguish logically between sociologists' discourse and members' discourse, as they see it. My reaction to the claims of ethnomethodologists would run, by and large, along the following lines: First, if common-sense understandings are inevitably used by conventional sociologists, they are equally used by ethnomethodologists; and second, simply changing the focus of analysis to what members take for granted cannot overcome this, although it can give an illusion of working without presuppositions. Third, the idea that sociology can regain its scientificity at the level of analysis of interpersonal relations is mythical, and not, of course, without political implications. Where the ethnomethodologists seem right is in insisting on the inevitability of using common-sense understandings. This means that sociology cannot claim its old-time, scientistic and early positivistic objectivity. But this is, to my mind, all to the good. Sociologists have shown a tendency to be either too grandiose or too petty, and in the end they have often settled for navel-gazing if not for the ambiguous role of classroom Machiavelli.

I know: it is always later than we think. And yet, we should never be in a hurry to conclude, to close the discussion, to arrive at a final synthesis. We live in an age, it seems, in which the lived experience is richer than conceptual frameworks. We must perhaps give up the nostalgia for a complete *globus intellectualis*; that is, for an all-comprehensive system, without renouncing the chance to build it when the time will come.

2

SOCIOLOGY IN AN AUTHORITARIAN SOCIETY: A Pessimistic Reflection on the Case of Spain

Amando de Miguel
University of Valencia

One aspect of the omnipresent crisis of sociology is the feeling that our discipline is no longer 'the science of society', but 'a knowledge of societies'. I stress *knowledge,* instead of *science*, because there is now a consensus everywhere about the multifarious array of valid methods and intellectual approaches, not always with a strict 'scientific' mood. I also underline *societies*, in the plural, because, for the first time in the short history of the discipline, there are sociologists working in almost every country of the planet, and apparently with similar afflictions. 'Everybody knows how to paint', Picasso said. Does everybody know how to make sociology?

I am very grateful for the critical comments of Jesús M. de Miguel, Benjamín Oltra, Juan J. Linz, Joan Estruch and Brian E. Carter; and for the technical assistance of Maria Carme Maltas. Access to several unpublished materials by Juan F. Marsal and Salvador Giner was also very helpful.

The majority of writings on the crisis of sociology has appeared in the few countries where our 'founding fathers' were born, and where a huge amount of research has been accumulated since then. But during the last decade an enormous expansion of sociology has taken place everywhere, booming even in the most remote and 'peripheral' countries. The assumed crisis of sociology displays different shades in those 'newer' nations. Very often imported sociology is diffused before its complete academic acceptance. Usually there is not enough freedom to investigate, and sociological output splits up into appeals for revolutionary action (not very effective, in general) or into sociography (mostly poorly done descriptions). At the same time the tradition of the 'classics' of sociology is found to be somewhat unrelated and difficult to apply to the actual processes of change now bursting forth in those nations. Moreover a state of chronic lack of communication with the scientific production of central countries is maintained by peripheral ones, only partially relieved through sporadic translations, private libraries, and round-trip academic forays of visiting students and scholars to world famous universities.

I would like to center the discussion about the crisis of sociology on a particular group of those peripheral countries, namely, those suffering (or enjoying, for that matter) authoritarian regimes. As we shall see later on, I will concentrate on the specific case of Spain, it being the closest and most inescapable example of my own professional and personal interests. Rather than a 'crisis of sociology' I would speak of 'the sociology of crisis', or better, 'sociologists working in critical conditions' everywhere; but especially in poor, authoritarian countries. That is my crisis and not only mine, I suppose. I interpret the crisis of sociology as something referring to the daily preoccupations which we sociologists face in our jobs, and not to the endless polemics about the meaning of the excerpts from the classics. If 'the crisis' refers to the polemics, I do not see much to worry about (at least in the context of this round table). There is no crisis at all. Hermeneutics is congenial to scholarship. No doubt sociologists' verbal anxiety is a little bit theatrical.

In analyzing the 'crisis of sociologists', we usually try to center our attention on the behavior of *other* sociologists, mainly those in power, well-established bigshots of the profession, leading figures from leading countries. This is completely legitimate, but not the whole truth. Rank and file sociology of our own brand also deserves critical attention. In the last analysis, every one of us should pass through the X-ray examination of self-criticism. That is not comfortable.

Following the 'reflexive' approach outlined by Gouldner, Dick Atkinson, in a provocative mood, proposes to break up the tradition among sociologists of not allowing themselves to be part of their exploratory task:

> That the sociologist should not be let loose on people without looking at himself is important. A few sociologists on the left are very belatedly recognizing this fact. But there is a tendency for them to look only at the sociologists on the right. They must look at themselves as well. Even the angels have a vested interest in a particular view of heaven and of whom Peter should allow through the gates, not to speak of how to get there in the first place.[1]

And his final advice, which I would emboss as a motto for my students, runs as follows:

> This, then, is the final request, that the sociologist should look at himself and recognize what he is doing, that he too is human and exposed to human pressure. This can only be achieved by the sociologist if he takes part in social activities and intentionally tries to change the world along with others. In so doing he will not only discover more about himself, but he will learn more about other

> people, about the nature and limits of co-operation, the meaning of hate or power or exploitation, and about love.[2]

If, out of the sociological fire that is nowadays so asphyxiating, we had to save one single valid idea, I would choose the following: it is not the same thing to undertake sociology (or sociology as it is done) in an industrial-bourgeois-democratic context as in an agrarian-traditional-authoritarian milieu. To begin with, to undertake sociology in the latter case, one has to take personal risks which sound like fantasy to the great majority of the social scientists living within the borders of the central countries. I do not mean sociology must be nationally-conditioned but something more straightforward: sociology *is* nationally-conditioned. Without co-ordinates of place and time we can hardly understand sociological statements, and this is even more true in the case of peripheral authoritarian countries.

Historically, sociology appeared in capitalist societies which had a certain degree of economic competition and substantial possibilities for representation and public discussion on behalf of the main social forces and interests. This situation is not always recurrent. Today in the majority of countries, sociologists have to manage in quite different circumstances. Capitalist forms are pretty much colored with historical and cultural traits, but most of them are dyed (and die) with intense state economic intervention and 'dependency' on central countries and companies;[3] their social pluralism is limited enough, and large areas within each country become 'marginalized' from their own central power, emphasizing the 'dualism' between developed and backward regions or sectors. Under such conditions, claims on behalf of a neutral and value-free sociology become quite unrealistic and unpopular. A 'voluntaristic' sociology succeeds everywhere. Scientific investigations are requested to help in many action programs, such as eradication of *favelas* (shanty-towns), birth-control plans, new towns projects, land or educational reform, and the like. The actual success of such projects is quite rare, but that is another story.

We must recognize that 'dependent' relationships have been found anywhere at any time. The new feature of today's landscape is that the number of real cultural and economic centers in the world has been reduced to very few, perhaps to two. That is why we speak of the 'Third' World as a unit. Due to this circumstance, many leaders, politicians, and intellectuals from these third world countries need to experiment with 'original' creations in the realm of politics, art or culture, in order to feel some sense of individuality or independence from 'central' powers. In that experimentation the desire for a sociology for transforming society becomes a necessary element.

The notion of sociology as capable of transforming the world and as never disposed to strengthen the status quo is something of universal desirability, but undemonstrable. It is one of those 'background assumptions' in Gouldner's terms, or *creencias* (assumed beliefs) in Ortega's terms. But social transformation and power strengthening must be considered not only from the standpoint of one's political ideology but also from the perspective of the type of country in which one is socialized. Both things stand out immediately from many sociological papers. The theme of *dependency* is a common feature of almost any macrosociological piece produced in Latin America, and this is just one illustration.

My point is this: there is no random behavior among sociologists, provided we take into account the country they live in and off. One of the variables that is nationally conditioned is the political system. More specifically, the meaning of undertaking sociology in authoritarian countries differs very much from the same operation in democratic-competitive countries (leaving aside, for the moment, socialist countries). Other significant dichotomies may be: dependent-independent, and central-peripheral nations. Each one may be considered an illustration of a complex set of variations. This is perhaps no more than common sense sociology of knowledge, but a great amount of thinking contrary to those observations is widely characteristic of many scientists. In order to defend my point, let me use the example of the Spanish case. Other countries may fit the model too.

SPAIN IS DIFFERENT

Sociology is a plant alive everywhere, like man himself. Sociologists shall be among us forever, but undertaking sociology does not mean the same thing in all places. Fruits differ in size or in taste with different climates. As Touraine says:

> The most uncomfortable situation for sociology is the existence of a motionless society, with a low rate of change and where, at the same time, a strongly integrated way of interpreting social reality is imposed on people.[4]

Curiously enough, Touraine applies this principle of the weakness of sociology to European societies (*vs.* American one, North and South), where there is an expanding rate of change together with a deep conservatism in many institutional spheres, especially the university. Let us say that inconveniences for cultivating the sociological species are especially visible in Mediterranean latitudes, and much more so in Spain or Portugal than in Italy. The sunnier the climate, the harder it is to cultivate our delicate plant.

The Spanish culture has several features influencing the late development of sociology. General poverty and widespread authoritarianism are only two of them. The persistence of a pre-modern culture might also be considered. The situation of the Spanish language adds a curious element of perplexity: being one of the major languages in the world (as to the number of people speaking it), most Spanish intellectuals feel quite secure in their official language and do not pass easily to other languages, as many Europeans from small countries do. That means a practical isolation from the creative centers that usually speak English, French, German or Russian.

Sociologists living in rich democratic and central countries do not realize these circumstances, as a fish is not aware of the surrounding water. In poor marginalized authoritarian milieus, things get more complicated; many sociologists need not only to succeed, to do research or to teach, they primarily need just to survive. This is not a rhetorical metaphor, but the plain, naked, literal reality. In democratic societies one can protest against the subtle devices of 'repressive tolerance'. In authoritarian ones one has to work one's way around 'repressive intolerance'. Let me quote in detail a past description of this repressive syndrome:

> [In Spain] practically every author of sociological books has some which have been censored; many of these sociologists have suffered long judicial prosecutions due to their professional activity. On the other hand, there are some who have been exposed to the temptation of participating among the cadres of political positions. These circumstances exhibit all kinds of tensions. The sociologist acts as wolf toward other sociologists . . . A social and political system bound to authoritarian tenets tends to forbid, almost by definition, the sociologist's activities, especially when he behaves outside the

> imposed frame of theoretical speculation or when he goes beyond the simple data; whenever those activities try to develop with a minimum of independence of the political apparatus.[5]

Intolerance of the system is absolutely compatible with friendly attitudes on the part of certain persons, even in the highest political positions, who not only tolerate but foster, help, and enthusiastically stimulate sociological activities. Authoritarianism is far from equated with consistency. In fact, one of its traits is unpredictability, i.e. incapacity to forecast in advance a normal sequence of events, due to a number of random (personal) variations. By the way, this makes authoritarian systems difficult objects of research for social scientists.

I would consider authoritarian a society where a large sector of the population basically (and perhaps negatively, passively) agrees with the decision on the part of the rulers (*los que mandan*) to curtail many 'civil liberties' mainly the possibility of regular elections, political parties and freedom of the press, usually in the name of higher national interest, historical responsibilities, and so on. Conformity arises in part from the hierarchical principle diffused among many other social relations, from family to school, from voluntary associations to work conditions. Obviously, the authoritarian atmosphere contributes very much to the predominance of certain classes, values and positions. The societal sphere recurrently reinforces the political one, and the latter in turn reinforces the social esteem of authoritarian personalities and situations. 'Those who command are always right' is repeated in different ways. Or 'our people is not yet prepared for democratic life'. Or 'democracy means corruption'. All these slogans, largely and diffusely internalized, are self-defeating prophecies as well as comfortable rationalizations for not giving up power, or not accepting changes.

In Germani's terms authoritarian societies would be those where *prescribed behavior* in political life predominates over elective or *free choice behavior.*[6] Political elections are just one of many illustrations. Referenda and elections may be frequent and fairly honest in many authoritarian countries; their peculiarity is that voters are compelled, through a number of legal and real means, to say 'yes' or to vote for a specific set of candidates. Voting behavior means in this case, approving, acquiescing, and not choosing. A similar scheme may be applied to other spheres of life, from marriage law to labor conditions.

Prescribed action sometimes means proscribed action: do not engage in political activities, do not attack 'fundamental principles', do not investigate certain topics, do not ask such and such questions, etc. Provided one can live with this set of prohibitions or regulations, one can enjoy an almost unlimited sense of personal freedom. But the prior conditioning provision is the outstanding element in authoritarian societies. The problem is that, in everyday life, ordinary citizens do not feel the importance of commandments to act or not to act. Everybody understands labor, traffic, sex, tax, economic and other legal regulations. Even industrialists, public officials, technicians, and professionals need not question laws and other social prescriptions. The contrary is true with researchers, intellectuals, writers. They do not always understand prohibitions or binding and forbidding rules. Intellectuals as rebels, or at least as not very convinced partisans, are found in every authoritarian country. Since they think of an innumerable set of controversial issues, they necessarily doubt, judge, choose, and evaluate, and consequently tend to exhibit a 'secularized' (not dependent from authorities) mood, an anti-authoritarian temper. Contradictory modern, urban and at the same time quite authoritarian societies may be found everywhere. Their only regrettable problem is that intellectuals do not fit well in such a contradiction.

Instead of 'intellectuals', let us put 'sociologists' in the former paragraphs, and the core of the 'sociology crisis' in many countries will be apparent. At least this is the best way to interpret the assumed crisis in a country like Spain.[7] The paradigmatic value of Spain may be an ethnocentric bias, the result of a personal selective perception more than an 'objective' outcome, yet I believe that what Gouldner calls 'personal or imputed realities'[8] are extremely useful in transnational round table discussions. Each of us comes from a different part of the world. Our intellectual input might be comparable (even the kind of academic activities we engage in are of similar shape) but the way we experience the *métier* of making sociology – whatever that means – is definitely unique and untranslatable. 'Roundtabling' is the established way of communicating such experience. Basic English plus a touch of professional jargon make up our *lingua franca.* Let us go on.

This personalization of my own standpoint does not mean that I consider one must be a Spaniard in order to understand Spain, a kind of monopolistic privilege. On the contrary, I have often criticized what Merton calls 'insiderism', the assumed privileged positions of insiders as observers.[9] In fact, a number of outstanding studies on Spain have been made by foreign *hispanistas* (Brennan, Carr, Kenny, Payne, Pitt-Rivers, Rama, Vilar, and many others). I understand that the Spanish illustration is just a drop in the ocean. One could argue that Spain has centuries-old universities or that she is one of the leading European producers of ships or cars, but that is quite irrelevant for intellectual life. The important thing, her peculiarity as a Western country, is that Spain is the very model of a peripheral, dependent (non-creative), authoritarian, though economically successful society.[10]

Spain is not only my country (the one that issues my passport), but the society about which I have collected an imposing array of data, both quantitative and qualitative.[11] Although Spain is so different (as the tourist slogan says) I realize that many other countries of the world, especially in Latin America, also conform to the model of authoritarianism-dependency-peripheralism-successfulness. One of the further advantages of taking Spain as an instance of a more general pattern is that, after all, she is a European nation, and that means a long intellectual tradition (though more of the humanistic type than of the scientific one). Sociology is by no means an article of recent import. Durkheim, Freud, Simmel, Weber and other classics were translated into Spanish no later than they were into English. But Spanish translations were not very influential on vernacular writers until quite recently.

Another peculiar feature influencing very positively the latest boom in sociology is the economic success of Spain, actually quite exceptional in the non-industrial world, aside from Brazil, Mexico, Greece, and a few others. It is a rare combination of miraculous economic growth with outstanding backwardness in other social aspects: education, land distribution, institutionalization of civil liberties and other bourgeois features, weakness of voluntary associations, and so on. This eternal contradiction is mainly a logical one or, if you wish, an historical one. This combination of authoritarian traditional elements with advanced technocratic elements is not absolutely unique in our world to-day; but it is definitely built-in, integrated into the Spanish system. A recent testimony of a thorough analyst of hispanic societies runs as follows:

> We have already lost the innocent view of the liberal positivistic sociology about the congenital antagonism between military and industrial society. It stands to reason nowadays that the objectives of certain types of neocapitalistic development are compatible with an authoritarian political system.[12]

In an advanced democratic society a distinction is often made between a professional, empirical, instrumental sociology and a critical or radical one. The first inevitably tends to support ruling class interests, or at least it does not question them, while the latter tries to help emergent marginal classes. In authoritarian societies things do not seem so clear. An empirical-professional sociology (although quite well established, in general) may be a revulsion against the ruling forces' attempts to hide many actual processes, facts or changes. It may also work as a trigger for making use of reason where irrational, emotional modes are dominant. It may question a series of traditional arguments legitimizing traditional powers. In summary, it may serve as a moderate form of change in itself. On the other side, paradoxically enough, a critical sociologist may very well be more fully integrated into the Establishment than the empirically oriented one (functionalist for short). The former is restricted to a limited and already convinced audience, and he is obliged to use a cryptic language. This cryptic-critical sociologist is eventually cherished by the political establishment, since he can be shown off as a token of the desired semi-freedom, provided he keeps within the convenient limits of utopian arrangements, abstract-methodological formalisms, or a mimicry of an alien treatment of problems.

I am judging neither the moral superiority nor the tactical usefulness (useful for what and for whom?) of each way of approaching sociology in authoritarian countries. Surely both are legitimate and stimulating. The point – the discredited point I must say – is that mere description of facts may be an important step toward changing a situation, where authoritarian rules prescribe ignorance as the best way of avoiding any challenge to the system. In the authoritarian atmosphere of a small country, being critical means to keep referring to foreign names, to abstract problems, to alien concepts, instead of dealing with domestic realities in everyday language. This trait facilitates what I have called 'international parochialism',[13] the astonishing condition that occurs in my country (as well as elsewhere, I suppose) where one can find complete sociological works on many critical topics without a single reference to other fellow-citizens or to concrete national problems. Of course, this can be explained in part as a mechanism of defence (how to keep publishing without perishing), but in that case it is a pseudo-criticism. My interpretation is that the behavior thus described is a form of authoritarian submissiveness plus a certain amount of ignorance. In reality, it is a way of conforming to the Establishment, of integrating into the social structure in spite of verbal declarations to the contrary. A more charitable explanation would be that 'one does sociology because nothing else worthwhile can be done' in political action.[14] This is the peculiar way of 'repressive tolerance' which is applied in authoritarian countries. Since the economic development is the legitimizing factor, empirical researches demonstrating the pitfalls of development tend to arouse suspicion. Since the power elite is usually not committed to a crystallized ideology, theoretical speculations do not affect the political creed.

Juan J. Linz stresses another limitation of critical sociology in a country like Spain: thinking that the criticized institutions are necessarily the most hateful of all, without realizing that they are merely the most hateful *among the set of institutions which one is allowed to criticize.*[15] The scapegoat syndrome, we might say. The final point is that a complete criticism never can be done unless one decides to leave the country, the simplest way of not doing anything as far as effective change of the political outlook of the country is concerned. This is an ambivalent result deserving a further analysis.

ARGUMENTS AMONG SOCIOLOGISTS IN AUTHORITARIAN COUNTRIES

Many of the features I am presenting here with reference to the painful situation of sociology in Spain may be due not only to the authoritarian climate but also to the weakness of the intellectual milieu. Of course, there is a clear interaction between these two processes, and it is not easy to ascertain which is consequence and which is cause. For instance, the fact that in Spanish sociology there is clear predominance of translations, comments, and exegesis of foreign authors over personal creations or interpretations of national reality may be a consequence of censorship, but it is affected by many other factors, such as the traditional focus of many university institutions (the routinized *doctorado,* the extremely competitive *oposiciones* or public examinations for getting a chair, etc.), the imitative dependency on foreign universities, the absence of criticism in intellectual life, and many others. Given this series of a factors a certain kind of Gresham's law is applied: lower quality works are easily published by the booming publishing companies. The consequences are a lack of originality, little creativeness, and a high level of personal conflict within the intellectual community. This picture is partially reproduced in other countries of the Mediterranean area, even in democratic Italy.[16]

A first distinctive element of intellectual life as produced in authoritarian countries, which affects what we might call 'the presentation of sociology in everyday life' – paraphrasing Goffman's famous title – is the following: in such societies there is a conspicuous curtailment of the public defence of interests through the mass media, voluntary associations, and the like. It is not by change that, given these conditions, many sociologists decide to appear in the role of spokesmen or opinion makers, something which would seem preposterous or futile in a democratic society.[17] One cannot interpret this role out of the context.

In many countries – obviously in Spain – a painful sequence of events recurs: each new generation of sociologists comes with Adam's complex, considering themselves as being the first ones to make the *right* sociology. I must admit that I myself have committed that sin of historical ignorance or lack of empathy. Some of the criticisms I have received are quite justified.[18] Like many others I felt proud of rediscovering the scientific sociology, an attitude quite far removed from the true scientific spirit, which is in itself insecure. In a country like Spain sociologists still have to argue with the representatives of 'traditional knowledge', namely, humanities, philosophy, natural law, ethics, etc. The political system needs this kind of traditional thought from the right as a justifying element. How can one dare to criticize it? On the other side it is also difficult to criticize some classical liberal (*arielistas*) intellectuals since they live quite apart from the official atmosphere (in fact, some of them live in exile); criticism of them would be interpreted as supporting the regime. This contradictory situation reinforces the prescientific knowledge, the low level of creativeness in theoretical activities. As a reponse to that stimulus sociologists pretend to practice a more *practical*, earthly scholarship. Frankly speaking, we have to admit that this position is a defensive one trying to legitimate the status of the new discipline. Yet its internal logic is not very impressive. Are our modern sociological exercises really more practical than the speculations of the *philosophes* in the eighteenth century? As a matter of fact, Las Casas, Grotius or Locke contributed to the understanding of, and offered practical options with regard to the public issues of their time much more than do their modern counterparts, the most outstanding sociologists of to-day. As a matter of fact, the influence of sociologists in political life – whether in democratic or authoritarian, socialist or capitalist countries – is much less than that of natural scientists, industrialists, lawyers, physicians, etc.

Perhaps the distinctive feature of a country like Spain is the lack of public influence of sociology even in intellectual or university life. In spite of frequent verbal declarations in favor of sociology, the true situation is that our discipline has an ancillary position in academic curricula. In a country where the university system is highly centralized and state-controlled (no difference whatsoever with the so-called 'autonomous' universities) there is a continuous abortion of the possibility of setting up sociology as a full university field, something which is both to be desired and feared. As an example of this ambivalence we may consider the case of the Report on Scientific Policy of the Spanish Second Economic Development Plan (1967).[19] This document selects four large areas of 'special attention' to be considered as strategic for research. They are: (a) sociology, (b) agriculture, (c) certain industrial sectors, and (d) natural resources. The outstanding place of sociology is astonishing. Nevertheless, in listing concrete researches to be implemented in the sociological field, eighty two projects are presented under the common heading of 'Humanities and Social Sciences', the majority of which refer to historical, philosophical, geographical, juridical, theological, and linguistic studies. There are very few projects on more experimental or modern social sciences, like psychology, education, economics or sociology. In fact, there are only two or three researches that can be counted as sociological, one of them sponsored by the OECD.[20]

Five years later, in the equivalent document of the Third Economic Development Plan (1972) there is not a single research project under the heading of Social Sciences. There is a working group on 'Humanities and Social Sciences' within the Commission of Scientific Research, made up of 29 persons, none of them a sociologist. This anti-sociological bias is expressed by official sources dominated by more traditional scientific fields. It may be that this reaction is actually a vendetta against the aggressive attitude of some sociologists, presumably more 'scientific', who try to establish sociology as the leading discipline among the humanities. I am not going to throw the first stone at those impudent defenders of professional territory.

In sociological arguments the attitude of denying scientific validity to others' positions is excessively predominant. Such an attitude seems more normative than scholarly, and it becomes a further obstacle to the development of an adequate intellectual milieu. This latter statement is perhaps too obvious, but it has to be stressed after a systematic reading of many current pieces of sociology. Ferrarotti suggests that the real argument is not between 'an assumed *Marxist-Leninist-sociology vs.* a *bourgeois sociology,* but between an *established sociology* – East or West – and a *critical sociology*'.[21]

I agree with that way of looking at actual controversies, but more precision is necessary. How can we define 'established order?' And above all, how can we determine who or what fosters that order? At least in the Spanish experience, a verbally 'critical' sociology does not seem to contribute very much to change. On the contrary, it is mild empirical analysis that may wear away the traditional order, simply by showing how things are happening in reality, how common people think. Let me give a brief example: in Spain a theoretical dissertation on the injustices, errors and corruptions of a generic capitalist society is more viable than a middle-range analysis of the attitudes of Spaniards toward birth-control practices. The former legitimates the established order in the sense that it may be presented as a symbol of the semi-freedom granted by a self-defined constitutional State. The latter discovers that reality does not necessarily correspond with the official interpretation of it, and that may be dangerous.

The major arguments in authoritarian countries are not between sociologies but between sociologists. The key test for predicting the degree of criticism in a given sociological position is not so much what is said but how it is said – and who risks what for saying it. Perhaps I am exaggerating slightly for rhetorical purposes, but in the early phases of an authoritarian system, where authoritarian tenets are strongly imposed, one can be more effective in transforming the system through empirical researches than through 'critical' analyses of a rhetorical and speculative type. I am not defending here many of the so-called empirical or applied studies – at least in my country – which are of dubious application, worthless, and often futile. But let me stress also that this two-decimal-places sociology I am rejecting is apparently no less trivial when it is done under critical or radical assumptions. This is why I admire so much those few critical sociologists in my country who love reality, who dare to come down to earth to do concrete research – and actually they are doing very well.

Norman Birnbaum has made it very clear that the usual antithesis between the holistic-radical results of theory construction and the partial-conservative findings of empirical work is completely misleading.[22] The conservatism of empirical studies is neither a principle nor a matter of definition but a matter of fact in concrete social realities. This fact has to be accounted for in the same way as any other fact. In most cases social investigations are directed toward maintaining and reinforcing the social order and the status quo (a euphemistic way of saying that bigshots never quit, and use sociological reports as another means of keeping in power). The reason: money for research always come from the top (top people, organizations, or countries). *Qui paga, mana,* we say in Catalan, which means something like 'Sponsors are always right'. Unions of researchers are not found anywhere. They keep talking instead of fighting against powerful, dominant and merciless sponsors. The day will come when some money for research will come from below (i.e. from people, organizations, or countries at the bottom of the social order).

We find a curious situation in Spain. There is an almost complete and uncontrolled freedom to initiate any kind of research provided the sponsor keeps the right to publish the final report. Due to the patrimonial outlook of many bureaucracies a great number of reports remain unpublished. That means a waste of effort, but also a certain capacity on the part of sociologists to undertake basic research using applied studies. This possibility is greatly reduced in those developed countries where sponsors know what they want. In the situation I am describing – basically referring to Spain – sociological production faces a number of miserable dilemmas, based on the contradictory claims that come out of an authoritarian society. In such a situation many sociologists, who claim to be critical,

a) have to be clear enough to influence political actions, but also obscure enough to survive

b) have to publish as is appropriate for an intellectual vocation; but publishing means at times 'selling oneself', 'integrating oneself'. The American principle of 'publish or perish' does not work, but 'how not to perish publishing'

c) have to avoid concrete problems (so as not to give the image of being 'nose-counters', 'marketeers', or what not), but to feel unable to contribute to the creation of original theories. Diagnosis: 'epistemological neurosis'

d) try to assimilate the latest methodological innovations, but being trained in humanities, law and other 'literary' fields, end up with rather descriptive, truistic essays.

A manifestation of these four ambivalences might be what L. García San Miguel has called 'critical conformity' as a peculiar trait of Spanish liberal intellectuals.[23] In any case, the solution is not a very comfortable one. One has to project onto the whole society the set of personal maladjustements. Even mankind is found guilty.

THE IMPORTANCE OF BEING MARGINAL

As I said before, it is difficult to separate factors due to the authoritarian culture (either political or social) from those due to the situation of 'dependency' of the country as a whole. Spain is absolutely dependent or marginal in the intellectual or scientific fields since very few original creations of universal value are produced by her. This has nothing to do with 'innate' qualities. Picasso was without any doubt a true Spaniard and one of the most imaginative brains of this century; the only problem is that most of his masterpieces were produced under the influence of the Parisian milieu. There are people who think that this phenomenon of dependency of countries as such is an abstraction, that 'all of us are interdependent', that not only industrial (central) countries are creative. I am not going to argue about self-evident propositions.

In my opinion this situation of cultural dependency (needless to say, paralleled by economic dependency) is basic in understanding the situation of sociology in many countries, and certainly Spain. In Spain, and in many Latin American countries, almost any type of empirical sociology is felt, in popular academic terms, to be a kind of importation or reception of an alien culture, similar to the 'reception of the Roman Law' in earlier times. The modernization of bureaucratic structures through empirical techniques is seen in each of these countries as a means of overcoming the difficulties of the capitalistic centers. Sociologists are accused of promoting *desarrollismo* or pseudo-development in order to maintain the subordinate, satellite position of their own peripheral countries. Whether justified by the facts or not, whether responsible or irresponsible, this is the main stream of the intellectual atmosphere in the Spanish-speaking countries.[24] Ironically enough, the one so-called value-free sociology is polemically involved at the core of the hardest political conflicts. We need scarcely be reminded of the 'project Camelot' affair.

Theoretically speaking an easy solution appears to be in

order. Nobody wants the worst for their country, nobody wants *desarrollismo* instead of true change and justice. The point is, how can one demonstrate that not doing empirical research is a help in demoting imperialist interests? Apart from guerrilla activities, what else can be done by sociologists in order to undermine or at least to precipitate change in their authoritarian Establishment? Is it really more advisable to refrain from doing research under the rationalisation that the money ultimately comes from the banks, and more ultimately from the Manhattan banks? These question marks indicate my own scepticism. Paradoxically, in backward countries one needs to apply social techniques to relevant, urgent problems. But since these measurement devices are considered alien to the national culture, and as channels of mimetic submissiveness to imperialistic powers, they are consequently rejected. Sociology tends to wild speculations and broad generalizations, ending up by mimicking alien theoreticians. These countries lack a solid university tradition, and truly theoretical creativeness is almost impossible.

In the so-called central countries it is feasible to rely upon a conventional division of labor by which most academics are dedicated to routines such as teaching from textbooks or nose-counting. A splendid, privileged academic minority can afford the luxurious task of creating, innovating, and advancing the scientific corpus. The only problem with this fruitful division of labor is that it is very expensive. In the peripheral countries there is not a sufficient basis, human or economic, for such an effort. Theoreticians by vocation have to undertake, sotto voce, dismal measurements, or, worst of all, act as local agents collecting data for foreign researchers from central countries. This role of a small backward country as a laboratory, or an illustrative case in point, for international projects on 'development' or 'comparative politics', is a sad feature of our profession; a strange profession, by the way, always begging, asking for generous munificence, and in this respect no different from one country to another. Social researchers are the mendicant friars of our age.

A further problem in many countries is the difficulty of importing sociology from central countries. Marsal discusses this issue with crystal clarity:

> In Spanish-speaking countries – by contrast with the Anglo-Saxon ones – science as such is visualized as something alien, having a devil's face. Everybody condemns it, either in the name of *los principios* (traditional principles) or as an imported product. This type of thinking has been very influential in hispanic societies, and is still the core of the rightist ideology. Recently the idea of a consumeristic *desarrollismo* (fake-development) has been assimilated with complete disregard for scientific development. On the other hand, we have the critical outlook of the revolutionary left for whom, to use a stereotype, scientific sociology is the last attempt of neocolonialist imperialism to elude revolution.[25]

Marsal points out the plausibility of both positions, rejecting professional academic sociology as it is practiced in many quarters. He also argues that the logical outcome is not necessarily the alternative of going back to the old literary essayism, which is perhaps a crazy idea in some developed countries, but something quite realistic in a country like Spain. Finally, Marsal indicates the contradiction in the outlook of the 'Disciples of the Left Apocalypse' who oppose by all means dependency on central, imperialistic countries, but who are unblushingly ready to depend on their own more effective and closer national regimes.[26]

The only way of breaking up the asymetrical relationship between the 'social-science-producing countries' and the 'data-providing countries' is by having the relationship inverted. Here is the problem: how to convince Spanish sociologists to go and study American society? A proposal like this would sound like a joke. Many (not all) would be ready to travel around the States; a minority would accept studying in some good American university (not for a long time, just enough to say that one has been there); almost no one would be willing to conduct research on American society, in order to convey anything more than a traveller's impressions. As long as this parochialism is rampant everywhere, I feel sceptical about the possibility of overcoming dependency in our field. We are dependent not only because they investigate us, but because we do not want,[27] or are unable, to investigate them.

THE LATEST FORM OF ANTHROPOLOGICAL PESSIMISM

On the basis of this analysis of the Spanish case, we may conclude that the crisis of sociology is, for the time being, the crisis of actual sociologists in specific situations. The most common attitude of all of them, everywhere, is a sort of professional frustration. We have been educated in a progressive tradition, in accordance with either the Comtean *prévoir pour pouvoir* or the Marxian praxis. Yet most sociologists – educated under the auspices of the Ivy League or the European radical tradition – have seen that their desire to reform the world through measurements or appeals to action are quite unsuccessful. It is not uncommon to see many radical sociologists making market surveys (and, by the way, sometimes with outstanding skill). That job is not as simple as it would seem; but neither does it produce an excessive trust in humankind.

Disappointed both with the institutionalized revolution of the socialist countries and with the childish tactics of 'our own younger revolutionaries', Norman Birnbaum concludes: 'Empirical sociology is largely a strained gloss on a reality we do not believe we can change'.[28] This is the basic anthropological pessimism we sociologists face after a critical self-appraisal of our work. Lack of faith in people is the essential core of conservatism. This is our main professional foe – not because conserving is bad in itself but because if we do not see change we shall not precipitate change. Everything alive is moving. Immobility is unmeasurable, and in its purest form is, in fact, Divinity. Much too far from our objectives.

Anxious pessimism is perhaps the peculiar trait of intellectuals. They always feel in crisis. Their criticism does not seem worthwhile since public life runs on as if they were not even in this world. If, by any chance, criticisms do have positive effects in correcting some maladjustment, intellectuals are ready to see the operation as a trick, as a conspiracy directed toward 'keeping everything as it was'. But restless intellectuals live on criticism as plants live on light. In a sense, being an intellectual is a disease, and since sociologists are intellectuals-squared, undertaking sociology is to live with an acute, chronic disease.

NOTES

[1] Dick Atkinson, *Orthodox Consensus and Radical Alternative* (London: Heinemann Educational Books: 1971) 277. The author con-

siders as a 'part of the crisis in sociology' the fact that '. . . sociological enquiry and exploration intervenes in and can affect its subject matter – real people' (276).

[2] Ibid., 278. Instead of the established name of 'social scientist', the author proposes the term 'active interpreter of social life' to identify the would-be role of sociologist. Playing with words, my colleague J. F. Marsal uses the denigratory expression *cientista social* (a barbarous literal translation from the English term but nevertheless, or for that reason, the accepted form in Latin America as against the more rigorous translation *científico social*) as labelling the old style abstract empiricist. Note that *cientista* sounds very much like *cuentista* a slang term meaning tricky, cheater, swindler (literally tale-teller).

[3] The so-called 'multinationals' mean *many* large companies from a *few* countries.

[4] Alain Touraine, 'Unidad y diversidad de la sociología' in A. Touraine et al., *Ciencias sociales: ideología y realidad nacional* (Buenos Aires: Tiempo Contemporáneo, 1970) 13. Written originally in 1966.

[5] Amando de Miguel, *Sociología o subversión* (Barcelona: Plaza & Janes, 1972), 73-75. For further evidence on political repression of intellectual life see my book *Homo Sociologicus Hispanicus* (Barcelona: Barral, 1973) 124-126; and Juan F. Marsal, *La sombra del poder* (Madrid: Cuadernos para el Diálogo, 1975).

[6] Gino Germani, 'Urbanization, Social Change, and the Great Transformation' 3-58, in G. Germani (ed.), *Modernization, Urbanization and the Urban Crisis* (Boston: Little, Brown, 1973). Germani uses this dichotomy to characterize 'secularization', a concept taken from religion (basically 'lost to Church influence') and applied to lay activities.

[7] For many details on historical and recent data on the evolution of Spanish sociology, the place of different schools and ideologies, see J. M. de Miguel et al., (eds.), *La sociología espanola de los anos setenta* (Madrid: Confederacios,n de Cajas de Ahorros, 1971); A. De Miguel, *Sociología o subversión,* op. cit.; A. de Miguel, *Homo . . .* op. cit., and José Castillo 'Apuntes para una Historia de la Sociología espanola' 104-144 in G. Duncan Mitchell, *Historia de la Sociología,* vol. II (Madrid: Guadarrama, 1973).

[8] 'What becomes personally real to one individual, then, need not be personally real to others. But whether derived from collective definitions or from recurrent personal experiences, a man believes that

some things are real; and these imputed realities are of special importance to the kinds of theories that he formulates, even if he happens to be a sociologist' Alvin W. Gouldner, *The Coming Crisis of Western Sociology* (London: Heinemann, 1971) 45.

[9] Robert K. Merton, 'Insiders and Outsiders: A Chapter in the Sociology of Knowledge', *American Journal of Sociology* (July 1972) 78: 9-47.

[10] Recall that the most academic and official interpretation of the Spanish constitutional system pictures it as a 'development dictatorship'. See Rodrigo Fernández Carvajal, *La Constitución espanola* (Madrid: Editora Nacional, 1969). The self-recognition of the Franco regime as an 'authoritarian' one is a recurrent trend in official speeches. On the paradigmatic quality of the Spanish case the required reading is Juan J. Linz, 'An Authoritarian Regime: Spain', 291-341 in E. Allardt and Y. Littunen, (eds), *Cleavages, Ideologies and Party Systems* (Helsinki: Transactions of the Westermark Society, 1964). In my opinion, a shortcoming of this exceptional study is that it leaves out many considerations of a purely economic or societal character, concentrating almost exclusively on the polity. As a result, important phenomena such as economic dependency (more visible in recent years) or strict authoritarianism remain obscured.

[11] Let me quote my last book, A. De Miguel, *Manual de Estructura Social de Espana* (Madrid: Tecnos, 1974).

[12] Juan F. Marsal, 'Los intelectuales espanoles y el post-franquismo', *Criterio* (Buenos Aires, March, 1972).

[13] Amando de Miguel, *Sociología . . .* op. cit., 17.

[14] This hopeless phrase corresponds, more or less, to the thoughts of Salvador Giner in an interview quoted in A. de Miguel, *Sociología o. . .*, op. cit., 73. Consequently Giner teaches at the University of Lancaster in Britain.

[15] Personal communication by Juan J. Linz. See Amando de Miguel, *Homo. . .*, op. cit., 25. A further development of this idea can be seen in J. J. Linz, 'Opposition in and under an Authoritarian Regime' 171-259 in R. A. Dahl (ed.) *Regimes and Oppositions* (New Haven: Yale University Press, 1973). Note that the Church in Spain was not allowed to receive criticism when it was a central legitimizing force, from the Civil War up to the 60s. The capitalist system has always been more criticized than the Army.

[16] See Edda Saccomani, *Gli studi di sociologia in Italia* (Milano:

Edizioni di Comunità, 1973), 17 and following. There are some aspects of Italian university life which are extremely similar to the Spanish case. See Guido Martinotti, 'Italy', 167-195, in M. S. Archer, (ed.), *Students, University and Society* (London: Heinemann, 1972).

[17] For instance, in Spain a good proportion of university professors in sociology are also regular columnists in daily newspapers or weekly magazines.

[18] I shall quote two brilliant critical reviews of my book *Sociología o subversión,* which, in both cases, is the work I like best of the particular author: José Vidal Beneyto, 'Sociología y garbanzos', 255-292 in A. de Miguel, *Homo . . .*, op. cit., and Ignacio Sotelo 'Sobre la institucionalización de la sociología en Espana', *Sistema* (Madrid, 1973) 3: 59-76.

[19] II Plan de Desarrollo Económico y Social. *Comisión Científica y Técnica* (Madrid, 1967), 12. The Plan is the official document containing the leading principles of the economic and social policy of the Government.

[20] Ibid., 85-86.

[21] Franco Ferrarotti, *Una sociología alternativa* (Barcelona: A Redondo 1973), 64.

[22] Norman Birnbaum, 'On the Sociology of Current Social Research', in *Toward a Critical Sociology* (New York: Oxford University Press, 1971), 214-231.

[23] Critical conformity 'is the attitude of persons who are more or less integrated within the system, and yet have at the same time a critical mood toward it, in many cases strongly rejective . . . Writings are, at the same time, means of conformity and of non-conformity; the published article may help in getting a chair and, at the same time, be an expression of our disagreement with the established society.' Luis García San Miguel, 'La generación democrática de 1936', 37-48, in Pablo Marti Zaro (ed.), *Las ideologías en la Espana de hoy* (Madrid: Seminarios y Ediciones, 1972), 40. The author is a prominent analyst of the political system.

[24] A fair interpretation of this trend can be found in José Medina Echavarría, *Discurso sobre política y planeación* (Mexico: Siglo XXI, 1972), 184-208.

[25] Juan F. Marsal, 'Sobre la investigación social institucional en las actuales circunstancias de América Latina', 87-100, in A. Touraine et al., eds. *Ciencias Sociales . . .*, op. cit., 89.

[26] Juan F. Marsal, 'Sobre la investigación . . .' op. cit., 92.

[27] At a very early stage of sociological development, we sociologists in a country like Spain feel a responsibility to study first our own country and not to dissipate scarce resources. We have a stock of missionaries to send to distant countries. The number of sociologists is much smaller.

[28] Norman Birnbaum, 'A Socio-Theater of the Absurd: The World Congress of Sociology in Bulgaria', in *Toward a Critical* . . . op. cit., 247. This article is a severe and ironic criticism of both the academic sociology of the West and the even more established 'pseudo-Marxism' of the East, as they were presented at the ISA Varna Congress in 1970.

3

THE CRISIS OF WESTERN SOCIOLOGY AND THE 'SECOND DISCOVERY' OF MARXISM

I. S. Kon
Leningrad Institute of Philosophy,
USSR Academy of Sciences

Modern Western sociology is contradictory. The post-war period witnessed an extremely rapid growth that turned it into one of the most important and prestigious social sciences. At the same time, however, sociology is being subjected to scathing criticism both from outside and from within the profession itself; and nobody in fact questions the existence of the 'crisis of Western sociology' that was proclaimed by Alvin Gouldner. What is happening in sociology?

In the view of several scholars, most clearly formulated by Raymond Boudon,[1] 'the crisis of sociology' is due first of all to such internal epistemological difficulties of this science as the vagueness and uncertainty of the object of study, the lack of clarity in the correlation of description and explanation, the insufficient rigour of scientific notions, and the absence of developed analytical theories. All these factors are, without doubt, substantial. But many of them are far from being new. In particular, the difficulty of distinguishing sociology by its 'subject' from other social sciences was exhaustively shown already by Georg Simmel. In addition to this, the existence of a methodological crisis is now being discussed not only in sociology but also in many other social sciences (psychologists are experiencing difficulties in combining the analytical study of separate psychic processes and the totality of the human personality; social psychology has discovered a gap between verbalized principles and real behaviour, etc.). And mentioned everywhere is the insufficiency of the 'traditional' definition of the subject, the sophistication of terminology, and the erosion of boundaries between separate disciplines.

In some respects the present situation is reminiscent of the situation in the social sciences and humanities at the beginning of the 20th century, when there was a fusion of such autonomous though interdependent tendencies as the ideological crisis connected with the termination of the 'peaceful' period of capitalism's development; the methodological crisis of positivist evolutionism that had dominated the social sciences in the second half of the 19th century; the revolution in physics and the crisis of mechanical determinism in general scientific thinking; the acceleration of the differentiation and specialisation of social sciences and the related growing interest in questions of methodology and, finally, the growth of anti-positivist trends in philosophy.[1]

The present crisis in Western sociology can be viewed from two aspects – the ideological and methodological. From the ideological aspect the 'crisis of sociology' appears first of all as a result of the disenchantment of a considerable part of the Western intellectuals with the dominant system of values. It is not accidental that the crisis of sociology became a topic of earnest discussion in the mid-1960s in connection with the left-radical student movement. This is particularly clearly seen in the case of the United States.

The professional sociology that was constituted in the United States in the nineteenth century was ideologically connected most closely with the bourgeois-liberal orientation. But the nature of this liberalism has changed. On the eve of the epoch of imperialism some fathers of American sociology (Lester Ward, Albion Small) were still criticising monopoly corporations, though extremely inconsistently and from petty-bourgeois positions. The ideas of social criticism, while not transcending the framework of bourgeois ideology, were clearly heard in the works of sociologists in the 1920s – (Veblen, the Chicago School, Robert Lynd). The situation began to change noticeably starting in the mid-1930s. On the one hand, this was prompted by the split in the left-wing movement that had gravitated to Marxism and the spread of illusions about the possibility of an organised capitalism. On the other hand, the institutionalisation of sociology and the increase in the proportion of empirical studies had weakened sociology's connection with pure ideological problems.

The natural process of professionalisation of science, including its internal specialisation, the appearance of its own terminology that is incomprehensible to outsiders, the growing interest in research techniques, etc., and in conditions of an insufficiently high culture of philosophical thinking, inevitably generates the danger of intellectual provincialism and of scientific activity turning into an end in itself. As for applied research that is intended to accommodate a particular social order, it is a foregone conclusion that it will be conducted in the interests of the ruling class. What matters is not so much the concrete political views of sociologists as their general orientation. The decline of 'sociological imagination' (Mills) and the tendency to turn sociology into 'social engineering' inevitably reduce its critical potential; and the existing system of social relations becomes not only an object of research but also a sort of established standard. This conservative-protectionist tendency was further aggravated by the decline of political thought and the McCarthyism of the post-war period. On finding itself shouldered out of realistic sociology, the critical spirit was forced to find refuge in abstract social philosophy and increasingly acquired an anti-sociological nature (Herbert Marcuse, Paul Goodman).

It is not surprising, therefore, that the new wave of political protest that questioned the rationality and immutability of the existing order of things, should also have come out against the sociology that substantiated this order of things, and brought about sharp discussions of the social value of sociological studies, criticism of the thesis of the scholar's political neutrality, etc. The point concerns mostly the sociologist's place in society and the functions that he discharges and should discharge, the criteria for the assessment of his performance.[3]

So this ideological quest revealed the untenability of the formula about 'the end of ideology', activated a philosophical and theoretical-methodological search and also drew attention to previously marginal ideological trends. But, of course, the crisis of sociology should not be viewed only as a directly ideological phenomenon. It also has deep epistemological roots embedded in the contradictory nature of Western sociology's development. When studied from within, the crisis of sociology, I believe, appears as a crisis of the illusions of positivist science, empiricism and functionalism.

The naturalistic orientation that was predominant in the Western sociology of recent decades did much for the development of sociology's research techniques and the sophistication of concepts. The progress in this field is undeniable. Difficulties, however, are inevitably engendered by the positivist conception of scientific cognition and the understatement of the theoretical and methodological specificity of social sciences. However refined methodologically, sociology lags far behind the criteria of precision employed in the most developed fields of natural science. Is this explained simply by an underdevelopment of sociology and its methods, or does sociology as a social science possess some sort of specific criteria of its own that cannot be reduced to the natural science ones? The rigid criteria of physicalism of the 1930s were gradually weakened even by the most consistent exponents of the 'natural science orientation'. The drastic intensification of the criticism of positivist conceptions of social knowledge, the underlining of its gnoseological and methodological specificity as compared to natural sciences, etc. constitute a characteristic trend of recent years.

The preponderance of the empirical tendency was a typical feature of Western sociology in the 1940s and 1950s. Although this empiricism was repeatedly criticised, many sociologists were blissfully hopeful and even confident that the increase in the volume of reliably established facts in combination with the progress in research techniques would sooner or later lead by itself to the origination of a 'good theory'. This naturally did not happen. Hence the drastic shift of interest toward sociological theory and, as a result of this, the revived interest in metatheoretical, philosophical problems of sociological cognition, debates on sociology's place in the system of social sciences, etc.

The discovery of the limited nature of the structural-functional approach, which was the dominant theoretical orientation in sociology for a number of years, also became an important component of the 'crisis of sociology'. The structural-functional approach in sociology is nothing but a particular form of the systemic approach whose methodological value is being proved by modern science beyond any doubt. But its application in sociology involved certain specific circumstances. While forming historically in the process of polemics with evolutionism and social behaviourism, functionalism brought to the fore the problem of the unity and integration of social systems. When applied to an analysis of concrete societies this methodological principle often developed into an apology for the status quo, an overstatement of the system's actual equilibrium and an understatement of its inner and outer conflicts and contradictions. While being good at describing stable components of the system, functionalism is much worse adjusted to interpreting crisis situations, revolutionary movements, etc. The notion of structural change within the framework of a definite social system is narrower than the notion of historical development. In addition to this, structural functionalism as a theoretical orientation is firmly identified in the minds of many sociologists with Talcott Parsons' theory of social action (despite the latter's repeated explanations that he viewed functionalism only as a language of scientific description and not a substantive sociological theory). Hence the notion that structural functionalism immanently lends a greater significance to value orientations, norms and other sociopsychological variables than to relations of objective social institutions, classes, etc. Having shown the profound instability of capitalist society, the social and political crisis has quite naturally entailed a crisis of the theory based on the idea of homeostasis. It is now being accused of lacking a historical view, of glossing over social conflicts and contradictions, of formalism, inability to reflect the process of originating the new that appears in society's life, etc.

It is this intertwining of the ideological crisis with the philosophical-methodological one that determines the present state of Western sociology. It is unfortunate that the term 'critical' or 'radical' sociology that is frequently used in this context is not very clear. The negative definition of sociology as being only a critical one is not enough for the delimitation of ideological positions. First of all, the objects of criticism differ, starting with the social system and ending with details of sociological research techniques. David Colefax,[4] one of the leaders of radical sociology in the United States, distinguishes four different styles of radicalism in sociology.

Participatory radicalism proceeds from the principle of the social responsibility of the scientist who consciously strives to contribute by his studies to the cause of liberating the oppressed and this is, first of all, an ideological trend. Cultural radicalism also proceeds from the sociologist's identification of himself with the unrecognised and the prohibited; but lying at its root are not political but cultural trends – counter-culture, experimental forms of community life, etc. Topical radicalism does not require a clear-cut political stand and boils down mainly to the study (often by very traditional methods) of untraditional problems for bourgeois sociology such as poverty, racism, imperialism and revolutionary movements. Fourth comes philosophical radicalism that concentrates attention on the criticism of the theoretical and methodological mainstays of sociology, first of all, functionalism and scientism.

These styles of radicalism are so different that any common platform, political or intellectual, is out of the question. Of the greatest interest naturally, are the works that suggest some theoretical-methodological alternative to the rejected theories. What, then, are the alternatives? The first alternative is often opposed to functionalism and is called interactionism or phenomenology. If functionalists, proceeding from the primacy of the social system, are prone to view the individual as a personification of the social role, their opponents, on the contrary, appeal to the interaction of individuals as a system-constituting factor. Dick Atkinson contends that 'a total model of even one society, in one historical period, is not possible.'[5] So as 'an alternative to a social structure' he proposes to create 'dynamic models of situations and kaleidoscopes' based on the interaction of individuals in certain historical situations. This 'situational analysis' means in practical terms the reduction of sociology to social psychology and this, though from somewhat different positions, was proposed long ago by George Homans. The trend towards the psychologisation of sociological categories is clearly expressed also by many other influential authors, Erving Goffman among them.

In my opinion this is not so much an alternative to the study of society as a system, as a different level of studying and explaining phenomena. Goffman's interactionist models are interesting and logical on the level of describing and explaining direct relations among individuals. But they do not explain, and do not claim to explain, macrosocial processes and relations within the framework of which, and in relation to which, there form the particular contacts and meetings among individuals, etc. They supplement the macrosociological perspective but do not replace it. This applies also to the so-called 'phenomenological' sociology that stems from Alfred Schutz. The social structure will not vanish just because in our mind we divide it into elementary inter-individual relations, actions of people and their intentions. The origination of 'generalising' sociology next to 'individualising' history took place in its time precisely due to awareness of the fact that the social whole cannot be reduced to relations among individuals and their motives. The criticism of reification tendencies in sociology, and the realisation that in the final count only living, concrete people can be the subjects of any social action should not, as I see it, lead to a regeneration of psychological reductionism.

Marxism is the other and really fruitful theoretical alternative. Interest in Marxism is now growing everywhere. More and more scientists in the West now admit, to quote Luciano Cavalli, that 'the Marxist analysis of the contemporary West is not only the sharpest but also the most influential one'.[6] Marx is being given more and more space in courses on the history of sociology, even those written on the whole from anti-Marxist positions. Also growing is the number of references to Marxist literature that one encounters in specialized publications.

What is Marxism's appeal to scientists who are looking for answers to urgent questions of our time? First of all, orientation to the *macrosociological* level of research within the framework of which, and in relation to which alone, fruitful microsociological research is possible.

Secondly, orientation to the study, in the first place of *objective* deep-rooted social processes and structures from which the facts of social consciousness are derivative. It is clear to all today that the distinction between the objective and subjective is relative, that one passes into the other, etc. But it is also no less clear that the study of social norms and cultural values does not replace research into the material and economic mainstays of the social structure, that although differences in the status and prestige of various social groups cannot be entirely deduced from their present economic state still, in the final count, they are derivative from class distinctions; that the study of the socio-psychological patterns of prestige and various methods of legitimation, does not eliminate the problem of the material mainstays and mechanisms of political power, etc.

Thirdly, the *dialectical* model of society with its emphasis on the study of changes, development, conflicting tendencies, class struggle, crises, revolutions etc., and not just on the mechanisms of the system's self-reproduction (though these are not denied).

Fourthly, *historism* in the interpretation of social phenomena. Isolation from history and the absence of a historical perspective most damagingly affect the state of the present Western social sciences. The faster the pace of social changes, the bigger is the scale of historical comparisons which is necessary for the interpretation of the relevant processes. The point is not the revival of 19th century evolutionism of which Marx wrote:

> The so-called historical development rests in general on the most recent form viewing the previous ones as rungs leading to itself and always understanding them one-sidedly, since it is capable of self-criticism only on very rare occasions and only in absolutely definite conditions.[7]

But without profound historical comparisons it is impossible to understand the nature of changes in modern society, be it the scientific and technical revolution, the socialisation of the young generation, or sex morals. It is for good reason that more and more articles, books and symposiums are being devoted to the problem of correlation of history and sociology and the historical method in sociology (as well as in psychology, ethnology, demography and other social sciences).

Finally, there is the *revolutionary-critical tendency* oriented not simply to studying but to renovating the world. In so far as 'critical sociology' is a science that studies the structure of society from the point of view of the ascending class and with the aim of this society's rational transformation,[8] it must inevitably gravitate towards Marxism.

But could this interest in Marxism be simply a new short-lived vogue? The present 'discovery' of Marx by Western sociology is already the second. The first happened late in the 19th century. Many leading sociologists of that period assessed historical materialism in a positive way. Speaking at the 1st Congress of the International Institute of Sociology in October 1894 Enrico Ferri even stated that 'sociology will either be socialist or it will not exist at all'.[9] Marx's contribution to sociology's development has also been favourably assessed by such differing thinkers as Ferdinand Tönnies, A. Small, and T. Veblen. Of course, I do not mean just formal references. Even concepts intentionally aimed at overcoming, 'eliminating' the materialist understanding of history proceeded, directly or indirectly, from the problems raised by Marx, and borrowed a number of his theoretical theses. Without note of this it is impossible to understand either Tönnies or Max Weber, Durkheim or Pareto, or Mannheim.

This 'discovery' of Marx, however, was a superficial and one-sided one. First of all, official science rejected Marxism's political conclusions, the theory of scientific socialism. 'Socialism is not a science, not a sociology in miniature, but a scream of pain', Durkheim wrote.[10] Max Weber and Albion Small, who opposed 'objective' sociology to 'subjective' socialism, expressed themselves in the same vein.

Standing behind ideological differences are also differences in theory. As is known, Marx's sociological theory combines an understanding of society as a system (the concept of formation, the mode of production as the basis of social structure, the principle of determinism, etc.) with dialectical historism (development as a conflict of opposites, class struggle as a means of resolving antagonistic contradictions, etc.). Now if the dialectical nature of Marxism is eliminated (and dialectics is totally alien to positivist thinking), historical materialism is easily turned into a variant of the eclectic theory of factors or vulgar economic materialism. Precisely this was done by the sociologists-positivists who mostly studied Marxism by reading not original works but various vulgarisations from which Marx had dissociated himself.

It should also be borne in mind that many of the most important works showing the dialectics of Marx's social philosophy (*The German Ideology, Philosophical-Economic Manuscripts* etc.) were published only several decades later, while Engels' letters on historical materialism in which he criticised a simplified interpretation of his and Marx's ideas were practically unknown outside of the Social-Democratic party circles. It so happened, therefore, that Marxism became known to academic science, ideologically hostile to it as it is, only in a distorted, simplified and vulgarized form. Such 'Marxism' could not resist any serious philosophical criticism and each new refutation consolidated the negative stereotype. It became a customary cliché in the West to regard historical materialism as a variety of vulgar positivist naturalism that had long been rejected by the development of science. Whole generations of sociologists, especially in the USA, brought up in the 1920s-1950s, simply did not know Marx's works, not to mention works by V. I. Lenin and contemporary Marxists.

The present 'second discovery' of Marx is, first of all, a discovery of Marx the dialectician. The accent is being put on the mobility, and the fluidity of dialectical categories, the unity of opposites, the understanding of man as a subject of socio-historical activity. This, however, also has its dangers. First, there are authors who think that the learning of Marxism can be reduced to the use of separate categories of historical materialism taken out of their theoretical and ideological context. Second, some people who undertake to speak on behalf of Marxism display an amazing one-sidedness and narrowness in its interpretation.

First of all, there is a romantic interpretation of Marx. The abstract dialectics of the young Marx is viewed in such cases not as a stage (important, significant, but still only a stage) in the elaboration of the theory, but as an intellectual orientation as such. And in the process the sociological realism of the mature Marx is dissolved in global formulas of 'total alienation' behind which it is difficult, and at times even impossible, to see the real social problems and the possible ways for their practical resolution (especially if the psychological notion of alienation is included).

The opposing of 'critical' Marxism to 'scientific' Marxism is also fraught with serious methodological drawbacks. The question 'Knowledge for whom?' that is often asked by sociologists now, does not abolish a number of other questions either for Marx or for Lenin: what serves to prove this or that proposition, what are the limits of its application, its heuristic value, etc.? Lenin stressed, in particular, the fruitfulness of the influence of natural science on the social sciences. Some young radicals refuse to study these questions at all, thinking that any empirical study means apologetics, while the refinement of methods implies a manifestation of positivist scientism. It is impossible to concur with this.

The question of applied social studies is many-faceted as well. Of course, the general direction of such research is determined by the interests of the ruling class, and sociologists must be vigilant about the possible use of their research for reactionary purposes (a well known example is the Camelot project which served as a cover for the activities of US intelligence agencies in Latin America). But does this mean that sociologists must reject social engineering functions in general? Is not the working class of capitalist countries objectively interested in the study of global ecological problems, energy resources, the age stratification or dynamics of the population? Scientists from the socialist countries learn with surprise from the works of their 'leftist-minded' Western colleagues that the formers' efforts to perfect the state system of planning and management, or to improve the moral climate of enterprises, turn out to be anti-humane and manipulative only because their practical recommendations are based not on general good wishes but on a concrete estimation of the level of productive forces existing today in their countries, labour morality, and other real conditions. A social engineer who is absorbed in technical problems can, of course, easily take the existing social relations for the only possible ones and thereby become their apologist. This danger should always be borne in mind.

Historism is needed not only in the interpretation of society but also in the interpretation of sociology itself and its history. Marx and Lenin, these unrivalled masters of ideological analysis, never failed to use the historical approach and held that the work of any scientist should be assessed both in the context of his epoch and in the historical perspective of his particular branch of knowledge. An analysis of a scientist's theoretical concepts should not be replaced by an evaluation of his political views and vice versa. Firstly, these views may differ in various situations. Giddings, an apologist of the capitalist system, joined in 1905 the 'Committee of Aid to the Russian Revolution'[11] that was founded by Maxim Gorky, while the Social-Darwinist Sumner opposed the Spanish-American War of 1898. Secondly, the value of scientific research does not stem directly from the scientist's political views, though it does depend on them. When the anti-fascist Tönnies is declared an apologist of the Middle Ages by M. Nicolaus[12] and Weber's doctrine of 'freedom from values' is thought to be close to fascism – this is simply not true. What is most important, it is not at all helpful in our understanding of the *sociological* doctrines of either thinker.

Some of the above-mentioned weaknesses of neo-Marxism are in fact revivals of mistakes made long ago and long overcome (for instance, of the vulgar sociologism of the 1920s) that Lenin figuratively linked with 'leftism, an infantile disorder'. Still they are quite dangerous. These mistakes could be put right by knowledge of Marxism's real history, including its Leninist stage and the contemporary Soviet philosophical and sociological literature. But unfortunately, Soviet theoretical sociology is much less known in the West than are empirical studies.

It is ludicrous to pretend that one has ready answers to all questions posed by the development of society and sociology. Many problems that are being discussed in the West are being debated in my country as well (the correlation of the systemic approach and the historical approach, human activity and social structure, levels of sociological research and the functions of sociology as a science, etc.). The further development of science demands a more vigorous exchange of information and the conflict of views that this entails.

NOTES

[1] See Raymond Boudon, 'The Sociology Crisis', *Social Science Information,* **XI**, 3/4, 108-139.

[2] See in greater detail: I. S. Kon, *Der Positivismus in der*

Soziologie: Geschichtlicher Abriss (Berlin: Akademie-Verlag), 1968.

[3] See for greater detail: I. S. Kon, 'Thoughts about the American Intelligentsia', *Novy Mir,* 1968, No. 8 and 'On the "radical sociology" in the USA', *USA: Economy, Politics, Ideology,* 1973, No. 8.

[4] David Colefax, 'Varieties and Prospects of "Radical Scholarship" in Sociology', in: *Radical Sociology,* ed. J. D. Colefax and J. L. Roach (N.Y., 1971), 82-83.

[5] Dick Atkinson, *Orthodox Consensus and Radical Alternative.* N.Y., 1972, p. 273.

[6] Luciano Cavalli, *Il mutamento sociale.* (Bologna, 1971) x.

[7] Karl Marx and Friedrich Engels, *Works,* vol. 12, 732.

[8] Franco Ferrarotti, *Una sociologia alternativa,* 2nd ed. (Bari, 1972), 7.

[9] Quoted from M. Rubel, 'Premiers contacts des sociologues du XIX siècle avec la pensée de Marx', *Cahiers Internationaux de Sociologie,* (1961), 176.

[10] E. Durkheim, *Le Socialisme,* (Paris, 1928), 6.

[11] See Maxim Gorky, *Collected Works,* Vol. 28, 417.

[12] See Martin Nicolaus, 'The Professional Organization of Sociology, A View from Below', in: *Radical Sociology,* op. cit., 48.

4

SOCIOLOGY AND SOCIAL INTEGRATION

Ivan Kuvacić
University of Zagreb

Sociology as a form of consciousness of bourgeois society has performed two main functions since its beginning: on the one hand it was *critical* – subversive – of the then ruling feudal system, and on the other hand it created the basis for *integrative* consolidation of new social relations. The former function predominated with the Encyclopedists, who cleared the ground and made preparations, while the latter came to the foreground immediately after the victory of the bourgeois revolution. The basic reasons for the relatively speedy acceptance of Comte's and Durkheim's sociology certainly include the fact that they considered that the function of religious instruction, at the time when it was being suppressed in state schools, could largely be taken over by sociology. In this the new discipline met halfway the interests of the ruling class, thus gaining ground for its own expansion and institutionalization.

By taking over from religion the function of social integration sociology inevitably turned toward everyday matters and the topical. In considering immediate social issues it was expected to offer solutions which would not divide and antagonize people but join and unite them. Of course it could not come anywhere near religion in effectiveness, and therefore it has sometimes been assumed that this could not be its proper function. The fact is that science, which is based on rational thinking and facts of experience, never can attain the degree of harmonious reconciliation of contrasts secured by the elaborate system of mystical eschatology. Obviously this is a matter of fundamental difference in approach, since rational understanding is set in opposition to mystical belief.

If we take a close view of European feudal society as a whole, we shall soon see that the division of labour and hierarchy on earth were justified by a corresponding hierarchy 'in the heavens'; that is to say, the latter was the final abstract level justifying all factors of social integration. In reducing everything that was and would be to what had been announced and recorded in advance, this ideology was effective and left no doubts until the feudal system of production began falling apart. It had developed a unique and comprehensive network of ideological institutions with many minutely elaborated and often subtle manipulative procedures. But the basic procedure was rather simple, since it could be regarded as pacification by turning people's attention elsewhere. The causes of all possible troubles are not real or tangible, therefore we cannot essentially alter the existing situation. But we can change our relation to ourselves and to the position in which we find ourselves. We do that by turning our backs on earthly troubles and problems and setting in the foreground such questions as: Where do we come from? Why are we in this world? Where do we go after death?

Sociology turns us decidedly back to mundane problems, and to their rational apprehension and resolution. It narrows in this way, at first glance at least, the circle of questions;

which does not however mean that it provides a higher probability of adequate answers, if they are to perform an integrative function. A fine illustration of this is Durkheim's concept of the social division of labour, which is topical even today, because it exists as the basis of the contemporary functionalist approach to the problem of social stratification. This approach starts from the premise that people in an industrial society will not accept and adequately fill the differentiated system of social roles unless they are stimulated in a specific manner. The stimulus starts from human aspirations and needs, which are potentially unlimited. If all people, however, had the same kind of unlimited needs and desires the complex contemporary structure of society would not be possible at all. Therefore society decides both upon the various goals for various groups and individuals, and the means which may be employed in attaining these goals.

It follows that the stratification system of inequality as such possesses essentially a motivating function, because it serves as a mechanism which stimulates the most competent people to perform the most important and most responsible tasks. Were it not for this stratification mechanism – that is, if rewards for all jobs were roughly equal – society would be inert and inefficient. Hence Durkheim drew the conclusion that the stratification system of social inequality filled an important moral function in two ways: on the one hand, it is shown to be objectively good, because it allows progress on the basis of selection and competition; and on the other hand, it can be considered good on the basis of subjective experience, because the division of labour should be viewed as the source of a higher type of human solidarity. In accordance with this view, Taylor's project of a thinking department, which will increasingly take over the function of management and coordination, allowing other departments to operate smoothly, should be whole-heartedly accepted.

But Durkheim himself realized that many features of modern development ran counter to his theory. He tried to explain this by the fact that a modern stratification system stimulated only those values which involved individual success, and the striving for individual success at all costs was the chief source of anomie. In search of a solution in terms of strengthening social solidarity, he therefore revived the idea of professional corporations, thus idealizing the normative order of feudalism which made everybody feel that his life was meaningful and fulfilling within the framework of his closed social group. Elaborating this idea, Durkheim argued that professional groups were the only ones that had the moral strength to curb individual egoism, to raise in workers' hearts a lively feeling of mutual solidarity, to prevent the right of the stronger from being applied so ruthlessly in industrial and trade relations. This was an anticipation of the idea of workers' participation and cooperation as a means of modifying and strengthening the capitalist system; an idea that was to reappear continually up to the present day. Individual egoistic purpose was mediated by collective consciousness at the level of the corporation. An analogy with feudalism is only conditionally justified, with the necessary qualification that an essential function was performed in feudal society by Christian eschatology. The attempts to establish an analogous corporation system in capitalist society, and to provide it with an adequate ideological mediation and integration, led to the formation of Fascist states, which did not diminish, but on the contrary sharpened, the disagreements within the whole system.

Thus the integrative sociological theory has led to the ironic conclusion that people must feel more free in a closed, integrated system, than in an open system which offers the maximum of individual choice and mobility. And perhaps more important still, this ideological about-turn, in its first practical forms, did not bring us any closer to the theoretically assumed goal, but actually drew us farther away.

At the time when the integrative orientation became predominant in bourgeois sociology, the impact of Marxist sociology began to be felt. As a projection of proletarian strivings and tendencies it did not pose the question of functional unity and social control, but started from the thesis that every society contains the seeds of its own destruction. In the same way as the Encyclopedists, in clearing the ground for the development of bourgeois society, were uncompromisingly critical and subversive of feudalism, so was Marx of capitalism. Having adopted a method which pays little attention to factors of equilibrium, but rather examines the transition from one form of society to another, Marx devoted all his energy to a critical study of the basic elements of the existing society. He did sketch the outlines of a possible, better society at the same time, but only implicitly, by the method of 'unsparing criticism of everything existing'.

The fundamental instrument of this destructive venture was his working theory of value, which he had fitted so skilfully within the framework of the general theory of alienation that it can be employed with certain modifications even today in conditions which differ greatly from those that he examined. This is because Marx's theory is not reduced to a dull analysis of rents, profits, wages, etc., but penetrates much deeper by emphasizing the question of the position and fate of contemporary man, whose basic qualities and potentialities have been degraded to the level of a commodity, an item of trade, a sheer means serving only the accumulation of capital. By contrast, there is a clearly stipulated requirement in Marx, not in the form of an abstract postulate but as a realistic programme, that man should be regarded not as the means but as the aim of production. This is the essence of Marx's criticism of the political economy of capitalism, and the key to understanding his analysis of the contemporary world; of which it is not enough to say that it is a scientific analysis, but much more important, to emphasize that it has a humanist foundation and starting point.

The issue just mentioned is the point at which the opposing streams in the sociology of the East European socialist countries clash with each other. There is indeed no doubt that, because of these countries' striving for a functionalist stabilization, Marx's epochal humanist vision is being neglected more and more in the sociology that prevails there. In accordance with these views the 'critical aspect' of analysis is denounced as 'negativism' which leads to anarchism, and the 'constructive elements' of Marxist dialectics are being strongly emphasized. This is the basis for elaborating a theory which is trying to prove that it is possible to revolutionize science and technology in those countries without changing other parts of the system. This means that growing material affluence should be aimed at within the limits of fixed social relations. This orientation inevitably leads to the development of powerful organizations, in which the increasing power of complex routine work is accompanied by decreasing personal freedom. The main proponents of this theory are the so-called techno-bureaucratic structures, supported by a wide and expanding layer of civil servants, highly skilled workers, technicians, engineers and economists, who are striving for a higher material standard of life and are not burdened by the norms of a revolutionary ideology. They demand higher salary scales and higher status as a prerequisite for a faster development and modernization of production.

In opposition to this predominant current in the sociology

of the East European socialist countries there exist minor, relatively isolated groups of defenders of the critical approach, and they lay emphasis on the necessity for continuous struggle against the conditions and consequences of a class division of labour, which obviously exists in socialism. In this way they articulate the aspirations of the lower strata of the working class, that is of the unskilled and semi-skilled workers, and also of some other categories of the population whose earnings only reach the minimum subsistence level. Claiming that global technological progress cannot be the only criterion of development, they persist in asking questions such as: Is there exploitation in our society? Is Marx's theory of alienation valid also in a socialist society? In their opinion, neglecting such questions means abandoning the standpoint of socialism, because there is a real danger that the vertical social differentiation in those countries might be distorted into a closed stratification system. This kind of sociological orientation, of course, is not equally represented in all socialist countries; it has undoubtedly been strongest in Yugoslavia, which is understandable if we bear in mind that it is closely linked with the system of workers' self-management.

It follows from this exposition that the sociology of the East is converging with the sociology of the West insofar as today both of them perform the function of social integration. This rapprochement is not the result of any affinity or transfer of ideas, but reflects the strong desire for stabilization and cooperation which exists in both systems. The same is true of the critical sociological trend both in the West and in the East. Its existence is not the result of an external hostile influence, as apologists on both sides claim, but reflects a desire for change. 'Functionalism going East' or 'Marxism going West', if taken literally, obstruct a scientific approach to the question and open the path for the legalization of political repression. We do not mean to deny any interaction of ideas, which certainly does exist on both levels. Thus it is quite obvious, for instance, that the functionalization in the East of some of Marx's tenets has been immediately influenced by Parsons and other Western theoreticians. If it is said that even in Marxism the initial and final unit of sociological analysis is not man but structure as part of the social system, the matter is quite clear. A paradox of a kind may even be sensed here; namely, that functionalism, which at least apparently starts from the whole, from the system, recommends the study of small groups, which spontaneously maintain order, while Marx takes man as the basis, and deals with large social groups which clash and jeopardize order and security.

This influence is not unilateral, since the viewpoint according to which the autonomous human agent is replaced by the environment has recently penetrated the social sciences in the West with great vigour. It is said that in normal circumstances man accepts only those stimulants which are biologically useful, but numerous experiments show that conditions can be arranged in such a way that man just like other animals turns his attention to one object rather than to another. A conclusion is then drawn to the effect that freedom and dignity as properties of autonomous man are obsolete categories.

This opens the field for gnoseology in the Anglo-Saxon world, and this gnoseology is entirely different from that which was established with so much elegance and wit at the beginning of the eighteenth century by Bishop Berkeley, and which found its wonderful confirmation two hundred years later in William James's theory of truth. With his thesis that for something to exist is the same as its being perceived,

Berkeley focusses on the autonomous activity of the subject. Claiming that there would be no perception if there were no world to be perceived Skinner inverts Berkeley's thesis, adding that the fundamental category of the social sciences is social control, which should be interpreted to mean that it is not man that affects the world, but the world that affects man. If we try to explain the genesis of this theory in terms of an affiliation of ideas we would not only discover that there is a considerable influence of the Russian physiologist Pavlov at work here, but could also determine that the most solid foundation for the above tenets is provided by the Stalinist reflection theory; but such work would not be of much assistance to science, because the fundamental source of the transformation should be looked for in the disappearance of laissez-faire from the American scene and its replacement by the mighty bureaucratic structure of the military-industrial complex.

There is no doubt that for the time being the economic and political rapprochement and cooperation of the two powerful systems are accompanied by ideological modifications and compromises, and thus by the nature of the case there is less room for criticism on either side. Just as in the United States and many other Western countries today the political and ideological attitudes of applicants for university faculty positions are much more closely screened, the same is true of East European countries, where many outstanding representatives of critically oriented Marxist ideology have had to leave their university posts, and this process is continuing.

If we should now ask to what extent contemporary sociology in the West and in the East has been successful in its function of social integration, the answer would not be easy to provide. First, there is the comparison with religion with which we started, saying that sociology has pròved to be inferior in this function. It does partly imitate religion, because it adopts established and unchangeable attitudes which are oriented toward the past, but it eliminates all mystical and eschatological questions from its field of consideration. This rational approach was quite convenient in confrontations with feudal ideology, but was revealed as fatally limited in situations where it had to create its own manipulative myths. The ideology of bourgeois liberalism, with its cult of individual freedom, which did not find it easy to cross the borders of national states, is almost completely discredited today. Marxism with its eschatological vision of a communist world, which required a return of man's interest from heaven to earth, had successfully countered religion until there occurred a gap between words and deed, and until there was a sharp clash between the Soviet Union and China. The motivating power of this vision has been considerably weakened today in the developed countries of Europe and America, which are now under consideration.

Therefore the view of the function of sociology as an applied discipline which assists the rational consideration and constructive explanation and solution of important issues of current development has prevailed in the West for some time now, and has already gained ground in the East as well. According to this third view of its function sociology is following economics, law and technology, in the wake of psychology which took this direction earlier and has therefore become a discipline of great consequence. Thanks to this function sociology is experiencing a great expansion both in the West and in the East. It conquers new fields practically every day, from the study of small groups, through studies of new activities, occupations and roles to investigations of global systems and the construction of futurologistic projects, where it makes use of statistical and experimental methods. This orientation emphasizes academic proficiency, which it links with the endeavour to achieve a neutral presentation of values.

No matter how well intended these efforts, it is difficult to escape the impression that they are to a great extent illusory. Empirical sociological research is not a noble venture for the common good of mankind, as it may appear to some young enthusiastic researcher, but is largely a component part of the efficient operation of economic and political organizations. This means that their scope and results are mainly calculated and programmed in advance. One must not forget either that the financing of such research is among other things a powerful means of control and subversion, exercised continuously by the centres and agencies of social power in the universities and other scientific institutions. Numerous research projects in the field of the social sciences, backed by substantial funds, are a powerful lever by which authorities can break the independence and fidelity to truth of many people in scientific institutions. It is not by chance that in spite of a rapid development of research techniques genuine research has actually come to a standstill; the great sociological investigations of the first half of this century, which laid the foundations for an empirical orientation in the discipline, stand as lonely milestones, which are often mentioned but seldom followed.

These considerations should induce a certain caution, in the sense that what may be presented as a manifest function of sociology should be distinguished from its possible latent function. That caution is supported by the fact that the expansion of sociology as an applied discipline bears witness to a change in the so-called global social consciousness of the industrial society, a consciousness which is decreasingly mystical and irrational and increasingly practical and rational. People are oriented to think exclusively about what is there, what can be computed and foreseen, and consequently what is strictly separated from anything that might lead to social tensions and conflicts. The age of the old ideology, which dealt in illusory fashion with questions of destiny, has passed, and has been replaced by 'practicism', which intervenes positively and discusses at length all possible forms and facets of human life, but always superficially and only apparently neutrally. The discipline adopting this type of analysis performs quite another function. It is that function which Simmel had in mind when he said that 'An equilibrium between truth and ignorance is essential for the social life of every country'. Sociological analyses and interpretations, moving in the plane mentioned, cannot grasp or discover the truth of life, but can neutralize it, conceal it, blunt it, sidestep it; that is, they may act as shock absorbers which by buffering rough clashes make possible a relatively smooth and painless movement along the predetermined path.

Does this mean that sociology has come to a crisis? An answer to this question requires that we should first decide the essential function of sociology. If we accept the viewpoint that its main purpose lies in serving social integration, there can be no talk of a crisis. On the contrary, in this case we should talk about a boom in sociology, which by establishing new relationships, holding conventions, and mass production of useful publications, is growing in significance on both the national and international levels. The main factor which not only induces caution but arouses antagonism to this view, is its ideological opposition to science, which is always revealed anew in any deeper scrutiny, in spite of mystifications and deceptions. Moreover, it is difficult to neglect the historical fact that sociology has appeared in crucial situations when people firmly challenged the existing social system: bourgeois sociology appeared when medieval feudal unity was decaying, and Marxist sociology sprang from a general crisis of the bourgeois view of the world. This is to say: in its original, authentic form sociology is a *comparative-critical reflection* upon the society, aimed at overcoming everyday routine by way of a thorough revolution of existing things and relations. This orientation inevitably presumes a perspective in relation to its subject, which means that its source is in the visionary idea of a possible, historically higher order of things and relations. Without a visionary basis enabling reflective thought to view what exists as doomed, there can be no decisive liberation from everyday economic and political rationality, and hence no overture to the future. As was pointed out earlier, this is not a matter of an independent flow of ideas in their relation to other ideas, but of ideas in the process of transformation into new ideas, movements and institutions; hence it follows that it is not enough to ask whether the idea leads to reality, but also the reverse, whether reality leads to a certain idea. Consequently, if we start from the latter, from the determination of sociology by the situation which has been outlined here in its main features, and accept the thesis of a crisis in the sociology of the developed countries of Europe and America, then, in accordance with the requirements of our approach, we must assume that this results not so much from the inner weaknesses of the science of society as from society itself, which in its basic processes is so much involved with mere growth and stabilization that without serious difficulties it blocks all the attempts at revolutionary transcendence involving qualitatively new potentialities of social development.

5

SOME REFLECTIONS ON SOCIOLOGY IN CRISIS

A. K. Saran
University of Jodhpur, India

I

Sociology is in a state of collapse; in any case, in a deep crisis. If sociology is the science of man and society,[1] its present critical state implies or presupposes a crisis in the soul of contemporary man and a radical disturbance in the modern Weltanschauung. In the development of this deeper and larger crisis sociology and other psychological sciences have themselves played a dialectically generative role.

The fundamental motive force in the origin and development of sociology in modern times – and there is only modern Western sociology[2] – has been what may be called the search for, and promise of, a new universalism. The crisis

Editor's Note: In the process of revision Professor Saran's essay grew to the proportions of a monograph, far too long for publication in its entirety in this volume. With his permission I have excerpted those sections which discuss more general problems (omitting the greater part of his lengthy analyses of individual thinkers) in order to convey some idea of his distinctive approach to our theme.

of contemporary man (and of the humanistic sciences) arises from the increasing hopelessness of this quest and the deepening disillusionment with the promise of a new man and a new society which the new universalism announced. This need for a new universalism is rooted in modern man's loss of faith in himself as the inheritor of a transcendentally given tradition and the bearer of a divinely revealed mission and destiny. Accordingly, it became an absolutely necessary condition for the constitution of the new science that it should be wholly and radically emancipated from the Judaic-Christian tradition.[3] It is in this negative ambition that we can see the fundamental principle of the modern Western search for universalism. The forms and levels of this quest have been many, but liberation from tradition, the ancien régime, is their common ground. However, loss of faith in the inherited tradition does not necessarily give rise to the quest for a new universalism or for a 'new' tradition. There are other logical possibilities. But because these, implicitly if not too explicitly, were excluded from modern Western man's consciousness, his quest for a new universalism has been inherently ambivalent and ambiguous. The course of modern history has, however, increasingly exposed this ambivalence and today the strains and contradictions in the contemporary world view have become more serious than ever. Indeed, today the very survival of modern Western civilization seems doubtful. Can sociology give contemporary (Western) man a sense of redemption from the burden of his own history? That is the crucial question.

With Western man's declining faith in Christianity, which roughly begins in the seventeenth century and comes to a head in the nineteenth, it was possible that the very idea of universalism should be abandoned. Indeed, considering the radical nature of some of the critiques and attacks on the

Christian faith, this would seem to be the more logical alternative.

> Feuerbach and Marx, like Comte and Nietzsche, were convinced that faith in God was disappearing for ever. That Sun was sinking on our horizon never to rise again. Their atheism both believed and rejoiced in its own finality, having, it thought, this advantage over former atheisms, that it discarded everything, even the problem which had brought God to birth in man's consciousness. They were anti-theists like Proudhon, but in a still more radical way; and they did not come to his conclusion that the existence of God, like that of man, 'is proved by the eternal antagonism between them'. They did not share his sense of the militant return of mystery after each attempt to overcome it.[4]

The most decisive aspect of positivism is, according to Comte, its tendency 'everywhere to substitute the relative for the absolute'.[5] Further, Comte held that relativism is inseparable from the conception that sociology is an exact science dealing with the invariant laws of social statics and dynamics.

Such an atheism and radical relativism should go along with what has been called historical pluralism, which consists

> in the view that the grand sweep of events which we call the historical process is made up of an indefinitely large number of components which do not form a completely interrelated set. According to this view, whether we take the historical process as a whole or segregate out any particular portion of that process we shall always find that in themselves all of its components are not related to each other in any save a temporal manner.[6]

At a more general level this leads to the programmatic injunction: 'We must do away with all explanation, and description alone must take its place'.[7]

Now this anti-universalism, in a variety of forms and with

varying levels of coherence, has frequently appeared in the history of sociology. The keynote of the sociology of the founding fathers was, however, frankly and unmistakably universalist. And it is the contention of this essay that at all times, including the present, universalism rather than pluralism and descriptivism has been the real message of sociology even if, at times, appearances have been to the contrary. But this is certainly not to say that the anti-universalist spectre has ever ceased to haunt sociology.[8]

II

Notwithstanding his programme of substituting everywhere the relative for the absolute, Comte is one of the clearest and staunchest protagonists of the new universalism.[9] Comte's thought is paradigmatic for our times. Fundamental to his system is the idea of the unity of mankind. He tries always to prove that there is one and only one type of society which is absolutely valid, and that all history must move toward the realisation of this ideal type. He isolates the typical features of industrial (as distinguished from military) society, and argues at great length that they represent the form of the social system capable of becoming universal. He tries to show that all human history must be viewed as the evolution of mankind, and draws the conclusion that the unity of the species is based on certain invariant (and universal) features of human nature. Behind the diversity of institutions Comte sees the manifestation of a fundamental order (of human nature). In a word, Comte's fundamental idea – the principle of human unity – implies 'a certain conception of man, his nature, his destiny and the relation between individual and collectivity'.[10]

Comte was the prophet of the 'first true revolution', an active protagonist of the emerging industrial society which according to him was destined to be the society of the future all over the world. For the smooth, non-violent realisation of this destined world-future there were two fundamental requirements: first, a system of scientific ideas which would preside over the reorganisation of society, and second, a new religion which would serve and bind the whole of mankind for all time to come. Comte's system of positive philosophy, especially his sociology, filled the first requirement; for the second, he founded the universal religion of humanity and proclaimed himself the High Priest of Humanity.[11] He also proposed that selected scientists and technicians should constitute the new priesthood of mankind which would exercise universal spiritual power over all societies. This new ecumenism was founded on his doctrine that all history is essentially the development of the human mind.[12] The fundamental law of this development is the law of three stages, from which it follows that only by synthesising all scientific knowledge and constructing a master science (in Comte's case, Positivism culminating in sociology)[13] can man lay the everlasting foundation of a universal society and a universal religion. The new universal political regime will be sociocracy, and religious positivism will take the form of sociolatry.

Comte's central concern was to establish a new universalism at all the required levels: philosophical, methodological, historical, institutional and sentimental-individual. This has remained the central concern of (modern Western) sociology throughout its development. At the same time, sociology today has also inherited all the unresolved contradictions and tensions of Comtean Universalism. The most striking feature of this universalism is that it is quite simply a Positivist transposition of Catholic Christianity. Starting from a radically opposed standpoint Comte eventually came to view his task as the establishment of a superior version of Roman Catholic Christianity.[14]

From this analysis of the nature of Comtean Universalism, it should be clear that sociology originated as a 'New Theology' promising to take over all the major functions of theology for (Western) man. It was to serve as a new cosmology, a new eschatology and a new soteriology. In what follows I want to show that in an essential way: (i) this original nature and destiny of sociology, this promise to (modern) man, is at work in sociology throughout its subsequent development; and (ii) sociology has not been, and could never be, true to its originally imputed nature and destiny and remains impotent to redeem its promise.

III

Marx is the other paradigmatic figure of our times. The main components of the major contemporary Weltanschauungen are common to both Comte and Marx. Evolution, progress, historicity and immanent teleology, anti-religion, anti-Christianity, unity of science, scientific technological industrial way of life, self-directing humanity, and perpetual and universal leadership of the West. The specifically Marxian ideas are: dialectics, inner contradictions of the capitalist society, alienation of man, class struggle, exploitation, revolution, dictatorship of the proletariat, and the promised advent of a classless society.

As a consequence of a combination of two sets of ideas,

universalism in Marx takes an essentially soteriological form, and social science is seen as a maieutic discipline. Marx shares with Comte the belief in the unity of history and the world-historical nature of the industrial society. But precisely at this point, difficulties begin. In sharp contrast to Comte and to academic sociology Marx does not regard the emergent industrial socio-economic system as everlasting; in fact, not even as long-lasting. For Marx this system, which he calls capitalist, has played a most beneficial and progressive role in the history of mankind but it suffers from fundamental inner contradictions from which it is destined to die before long. It is only after the end of capitalist industrialism that freedom reigns and world history properly begins.

To accept Marxism is to be committed to a specific 'ontology', epistemology, ethics and social science. It is a complete world-view and logically demands individual allegiance. But in contrast to metaphysics and theology the fundamental perspective of Marxian thought is anthropological. It is in terms of anthropology that his entire system is constructed. 'We recognize' says Marx in *The German Ideology*, 'only one science, the science of history'.[15] Henri Lefebvre interprets this as follows:[16] by historical reality, or 'historicity', we denote the process by which man is formed, what he produces (in the broadest and strongest sense) by himself, through his practical activity. Man is born of nature; he comes into being, he emerges, he asserts himself. What he becomes is the result of his own efforts, of his struggle against nature and against himself. In the course of this dramatic process, forms and systems make their appearance. The formation of social man, like that of biological man, is marked by periods of relative stability, relatively stable structure. These too are eventually drawn into the process of change, are sooner or later dissolved or destroyed, yet they endured for a time, they were part of history, and deserve to be studied for their own sake. Man, both as individual and as member of society, thus comes to look upon himself as a historical being. His essence is historical and unfolds within history; he constitutes, creates, produces himself in the domain of praxis.

This history is not to be opposed to nature though it may be distinguished from the evolution of nature after a certain stage. Man and Nature are both the product of a universal and unending movement. The emergence of man is, however, an absolutely unique (i.e. unprecedented and by virtue of its nature, unsurpassable) moment in this history. With the emergence of man, the process becomes conscious of itself, and at another stage of what may now be called the man-nature-society movement man becomes conscious of the process as a whole and thus gains the potentiality for achieving complete mastery over it. This is also the moment when man becomes aware that he is a self-created being. Marxian man has thus a double aspect: as the creature (product) of the historical process and as the master of nature and human history. Marx's theory of the relationship between these two aspects is, I think, the essence of his world view.

Man develops by opposing

> himself to Nature as one of her own forces, setting in motion arms and legs, head and hands, the natural forces of his body in order to appropriate Nature's product in a form adapted to his own needs. Only by acting on the external world and changing it, he at the same time changes his own nature. He develops his slumbering powers and compels them to act in obedience to his sway.[17]

This process necessarily involves a plurality of men, and the interaction between man and nature determines the form of human association. From this process emerge simultaneously two originally related but distinguishable structures, which may be called the social (man-man relationship) and the economic (man-nature relationship).

All through history (natural and human) disharmonies are created at one stage and resolved at another. In the specifically human phase this disharmony appears in the form of an eventually antagonistic pattern of development of the two structures, social and economic-technical, culminating in the capitalist mode of production of our own times. This mode of production is again absolutely unique and of crucial significance in the history of man:

> We see here the universal tendency of capital which distinguishes it from all earlier stages of production. Although it is itself limited by its own nature, capital strives after the universal development of productive forces, and this becomes the prerequisite for new means of production. This tendency . . . distinguishes capital from all earlier means of production, and contains the implication of its own transitory nature.[18]

This gives us the universal destiny of man; namely, to plan, lead and control the transition from present-day society, the last form of antagonistic societies, to the future communist society in which 'men liberated from the "alienations" and "mediations" of capitalist society, would be the masters of their own destiny through their understanding and control both of nature and their own social relationships'.[19]

This, however, gives us only the destiny of contemporary man. How about the man of the future? In Marx, man has two faces: man the labourer, and man the scientist (the conqueror of nature and master of history). According to Marx, however these are not two natures of man but simply two aspects of a single nature. If this is to be so, either the essence of man's nature should transcend both aspects, or one of the two should be the essence. Now, inverting the traditional hierarchy of *vita contemplativa* and *vita activa,* Marx recognizes only the latter. Here too, he really recognizes only labour and defines man in terms of it; indeed, man himself is created by labour. 'Labour is the eternal natural necessity to effect the metabolism between man and nature'.[20] But man is not just a labouring animal: what distinguishes him from all other species is that he 'owns' surplus labour-power, that is to say, the energy that remains after he has been able, through his own labour, to reproduce himself. In the Marxian system, this surplus labour-power of man is, in the last analysis, the only source of all development. The basic self-destruct mechanism that Marx finds at the heart of different historical regimes, most particularly in contemporary capitalist society, is simply the bondage, in one form or another, of this immense human power. Exploitation of man by man at the socio-economic level, and alienation at the human level, are the most significant forms of the present mode of its bondage. It follows that in the Marxian system, man the scientist must necessarily be seen as the positive transformation of the (surplus) labour power of man.

The new eschaton of man as defined in Marxism has been described as the transition to the non-exploitative, non-antagonistic post-capitalist society ('socialized humanity', the 'reign of freedom', the beginning of truly 'human history') and simultaneously as the transition from the alienated to the integrated man. Such a regime is to be seen not merely as one social type among others; but as the very telos of 'mankind's search for itself'.

It is, however, possible to give another formulation in terms of the complete emancipation of human labour power. This has been taken to mean the abolition of the necessity to work. For Marx, this means that the liberated labour power will automatically nourish higher activities of man. The two formulations are in certain significant ways divergent; but both are found in Marx, who perhaps would dismiss the problem of divergence between the two as an example of undialectical or mechanistic thinking. The latter version, in terms of the emancipation of labour power, however, implies a more far-reaching destiny for man. In thus proclaiming a new world view, or the first ever universal world view, Marx totally rejects all the received religious world views. In the future communist society there will hence be no need for religion nor for any substitute for it.

Do these teachings constitute the basic Marxist sociology? Perhaps they do not. Following current jargon they may be said to constitute a sort of (Marxist) metascience; in an older terminology they are first principles. Marxist sociology will essentially be the analysis of the transitory capitalist society; founding itself, of course, on the above principles and proceeding always in terms of the above methodology and framework of concepts. The task of sociology will be to function as an instrument of the Revolution. The nature of Marxian universalism can now be summed up. First it proclaims the universality of the industrial society (based on the projected universal supremacy of modern science and technology), and the consequent universal proletariat, universal revolution and non-exploitative society as the universal future. All this assumes the validity of the Comtean postulate of the unity of history. Second, Marxism proclaims a method of analysis and interpretation both of nature and human history which is of universal application and validity. Third, Marxism proclaims a common *'eschaton'* for all societies, a universal meaning for human life and a common destiny for contemporary man.

IV

Max Weber, it may be said, continued to believe in the world-historical destiny of European man. And this implies the universalism of the industrial-technological society. Perhaps he did; but it was with resignation, not with any assurance or enthusiasm, that he thought of the future. For it was with deep anguish that he observed the double face of rationalisation, and he could not but see the anomic and dehumanising forces as central rather than peripheral to the modern socio-cultural system. If the encyclopaedic scholarship of Weber thus failed to provide a positive sociological *summa,* this does not imply a personal failure. It means simply and clearly that social science henceforward could only be social criticism; if even that, for sound social criticism assumes an accepted social philosophy. The days of 'positive philosophy' were over. More ominously, Weber's pessimism reflects the progressive weakening of the élan that had sustained so long the social science Weltanschauung against its inner contradictions and strains.

More than half a century separates Weber's time from our own, and these decades have been the time when sociology has grown steadily and rapidly, matured, and according to many of its protagonists, come of age. Except during the last decade any talk of a crisis in sociology (to say nothing of its end) would have sounded eccentric, even crazy. As late as 1970, Gouldner speaks only of the coming crisis of Western sociology. The anguish of Weber's thinking left no significant trace in mainstream sociology as it developed in America and England in the post-1918 period. There are only faint echoes, if any, of the despair and disenchantment, of the insensitivity and excess of a sensate culture, of the schism in the soul of man. Latter-day sociologies reflect, in various direct and oblique ways, the small personal faiths of Weber, Sorokin and Toynbee: recovery of the greatness of Germany, renaissance of creative altruism, renewal of Christianity and the Communion of Saints – all variations of Comtean motifs.

The development of sociology between the two world wars and particularly after the second world war is a strange phenomenon. The utterly shattering experience of the war, of Hiroshima, of cold war, of nuclear terror, of impending global ecological disaster, find no central structural expression in mainstream sociological thinking. There are, of course, technical discussions of nuclear symmetry and the balance of terror, and of 'post-modern' and 'post-industrial society', but no human concern. The strangest thing is that in spite of modern sociology's near obsessive appreciation of the newness, the uniqueness, of our times, the terrifying, world-destroying newness of nuclear technology is regularly and insistently denied. Every effort is made to assimilate it to previous technological revolutions: the invention of gunpowder, the transformation of agriculture. I do not know the correct explanation for this incredible falsification of contemporary Western man's consciousness. (If I speak here only of Western man's consciousness, it is for the simple reason that non-Western consciousness – say, the consciousness of contemporary India – is no more and no less than the obsolescent projection of the Western.)

The end of formal and political imperalism, and the emergence of the USA and the USSR as nuclear superpowers, make the development and modernization of the underdeveloped Third World the major (perhaps the only) concern of American sociology. Even Europe has to modernize, and the question whether this means the 'Americanization of Europe' becomes an important one. 'Modernization' is now the mode in which universalism finds expression. It works as a substitute for the lost élan of Western man and helps him to falsify his experience of war and blunt his sense of the inner collapse of his civilization. At different levels and in various ways, sociology today reflects and reinforces this new consciousness.

The development of the idea and the institution of the Welfare State after the first world war is also closely connected with the character of recent sociology. The Welfare State creates for the sociologist a situation in which he has to make a radical decision: either he has to work for the destruction of the (liberal) industrial-technological society, in which case, the whole of modern sociology becomes irrelevant and has to be renounced; or he works for the strengthening of the Welfare State, in which case, he becomes essentially a social engineer, or perhaps more correctly, a public relations expert for the state.

V

It would be useful to regard the development of sociology as being divided into two periods. In the earlier phase of its founding fathers, sociology was the science and philosophy (or, from another standpoint, the ideology) of technological-industrial society. Its central concern, accordingly, was to overcome hostile forces and elements of uncertainty, and to establish firmly the capitalist industrial society in Europe, giving a peaceful burial to the feudal-military society. This, with appropriate modifications, could also be said to be the role of sociology in America. In its later phase, which begins after the first world war and comes to maturity during the sixties, sociology looks upon industrial society as firmly established in the West. (The challenge of Communist society however remains an acute embarrassment.) Europe and America have already been modernized and sociology has rendered the required service in this transformation. Its new mission is to establish 'scientific-technological' societies in the rest of the world and thus modernize it. The difference between the two outlooks is not that the latter has a world mission, while the former confines itself to Europe only. This certainly is not true. The point is that in the earlier phase, Europe itself was the candidate for industrialization; and, moreover, European imperialism and colonization in Asia, Africa and the Americas were taking care of the world mission of sociology at another and more powerful level.

In a broad sense, post-1918 mainstream sociology took the American model of industrial-technological society to be a permanently valid and valuable one. This being so, sociology during this time devoted itself to elaborating theories and concepts which were based on interpretations of the existing American society – economic, political and religious-cultural systems and certain non-social-science belief-systems accompanying or underlying them. These were simply assumed to be, in principle, true of any social system, past, present and future; and it was believed that while accumulated empirical knowledge would, in the course of time, modify theoretical generalization, empirical sociological investigations could use the existing principles of sociology as their theoretical framework. It was also the unexpressed hope that somehow only marginal modifications would be necessary in the fundamental principles of sociology. It is in this way that socialization, social processes (competition, co-operation, accommodation, assimilation, etc.), social differentiation and stratification, social change, social control, heredity, environment, groups, states, institutions, folkways etc., were treated in sociology textbooks. Even if some of the features of ancient or primitive societies may differ fundamentally from modern Western society, these can be treated as deviations, exceptions or extreme points which prove rather than refute the generality of these principles and categories. (Hierarchy can be treated as a special case in stratification theory, caste can be seen as a closed class, and so on). In this way, textbook (scientific) sociology claimed independence of universal history, disdaining to concern itself with the nature and ultimate destiny of man and his community life, refusing to worry about the distant future except in the pragmatic mode and on behalf of the present.

The basis of this scientific sociology was, of course, neither conceptual generality, nor any new stoicism, but simply the absolutisation of the American way of life (whatever that may mean), or at best of the Western scientific industrial way of life. This fiction of scientific sociology has been maintained by a threefold ethnocentric assumption: (i) the West is the centre of the universe; (ii) the modern Western way of life is the meaning and end of human history, and time comes to a stop with the maturation of this form of human social life; (iii) human consciousness can be reduced to the psychology of Western man's history.

In order to escape such assumptions of contemporary scientific empiricism, which claims to overcome metaphysics by social science, another device is sometimes adopted. It is declared that sociology at the present stage of its development cannot provide general principles of any great scope. Through empirical and comparative investigations it is accumulating material on the basis of which a body of universal generalizations will one day be constructed. Meanwhile sociology investigates the major problems of Western society and the sociologist can serve the society as an engineer, solving problems piecemeal. He is not, and at this stage cannot be, a *mustafa mond,* a prophet, or a priest; nor yet can he be a revolutionary committed to the inauguration of a new universal social order.

This view is, of course, founded on what may be called methodological universalism. Without it no scientific microsociology, however cautious and limited in scope, can start at all. Besides the methodology of Comtean sociology, or of Parsonian grand theory, we have a number of methodologies: scientific empiricism, logical empiricism, structural-functionalism (including role theory), phenomenological analysis, exchange theory, the hermeneutical method, and so on.[21] These involve two sets of problems. Scientific and logical empiricisms assume that a single method designed for the study of nature can be applied to the study and understanding of human society and culture. This master postulate, however, involves a belief that there are different methodologies for, say, life and ecological sciences, but nevertheless, there is a core scientific method which is common to both the natural and the social sciences. Again there is a two-fold implication: (i) that the core scientific method can be applied to all types of societies, or (ii) that a particular scientific method, say, the methodology of structural biology or the cybernetic method, alone is so applicable. Alternatively, it may be held that some methodology, say, that of life science, is suited to one type of society, another to a different type of society. The state of the art in contemporary microsociology is definitely confused. To clear up these confusions and to make a well-founded logical-dialectical decision among the several possibilities mentioned above would be to make the transition from methodological to substantive universalism.

Other methodologies make an opposite assumption;

namely, that scientific method in sociology cannot be the same as in the natural sciences. Here two views are possible: (i) that the same methodology is feasible for the study and understanding of all societies; and (ii) that different methods are needed for different societies and that a unified cultural sciences methodology is impossible. Both views, however, reject the evolutionary philosophy of history and thus the Comtean school.

Now this independence of history implies a timeless perspective which cannot be formally accepted by modern sociology or anthropology because its full metaphysical implications are diametrically opposed to its original spirit and basic principles. As a universal method it might be defined as follows: the sociologist tries to discover the immanent teleology of a social system and then studies how the system maintains itself. Sociology is thus concerned simply with providing an understanding of how a social system, any social system, maintains itself. It is presupposed here that all societies are self-maintaining and self-correcting systems. This is obviously a substantive generalization of the widest scope and is neither simple nor unquestionable.

I will raise here only the following points. Ernest Gellner says that

> the historic service performed by the shock of timelessness introduced by Malinowski was to make people into structuralists: when they become structuralists, they could then cease to be timeless.[22]

The functionalist analysis, he says, can be applied to unstable situations just as much as to stable ones; and it 'in no way requires a rejection either of change and development or of concern with the past'.[23] This seems too good to be true; for as soon as the structuralist-functionalist method is applied to the understanding of unstable systems, there are, in terms of this method, two and only two options: the system is moving either toward decadence and death, or toward reintegration at a different level. In the latter case a philosophy of history is clearly involved. In the former case, the second option has to be eliminated, and the immanent teleology of the system discovered; both these endeavours are essentially problematic.

VI

Recent sociology has been in a highly self-critical phase vis à vis Comtean universalism. One major aspect of it, however, has been unmistakably universalist: namely, the theory of modernization and social change. In the theory of modernization the crisis of sociology today is expressed in one of its quintessential forms; and yet, except for a small minority of thinkers, it is here that sociology looks most self-confident and irresistible.

Modernity is a time-word, but it is always used as a quality-word. It has to be so because, except in a few specific contexts, a purely descriptive use of words becomes trivial, so that all periodizations imply evolution; and second because an axiological use of the concept of time is a central implication of the idea of Progress which has dominated our age.

> The consequence of a belief in progress . . . is that time ceases to be morally neutral. A society can be said to believe in progress . . . when there is, at the very least, some prediposition to tie up *past* with *bad* (in one word: backward), and *future* with *good* (progressive) . . . In some milder sense at any rate, it seems obvious that European thought since the eighteenth century has come to assume the idea of progress, and, indeed, that the idea has come to permeate

> ordinary thought and be built into its assumptions and languages. . . Life has come to be lived *on an upward slope.*[24]

Now this axiological concept of time conflicts with two other basic beliefs of our time: positivism and historicism, although these two beliefs are supposed to reinforce each other. It is argued that to use modernity as a quality-word is not to violate the value-neutrality that is associated with positive (scientific) sociology, because the values of modernity (and hence the value of modernity) are given by history itself. Positivism or science is not neutral to all values but only to ahistorical, non-scientific ones. Both logically and historically this argument is unsound. Logically, comparative history leads one to value relativism and historical pluralism, and from that point of view, the question of modernization just does not arise. In other words, modernity cannot be used as a quality-word without freezing a portion of history; and this absolutization of a fragment is so patently anti-historical that it is a miracle that no serious attention has been paid to this problem. If there have to be any absolute values validated by history, time must have a stop; and time, for our modern sociologists, does have a stop. To see this, one must know that though the sociology of modernization and social change pretends to be universal in validity and global in scope, it is meant exclusively for the low development countries (LDCs), and does not apply at all to North America and Europe. For them there may be problems of post-industrial, post-modern, or post-Christian society, but these are radically different from the problems and dilemmas of modernization in the low development countries. For Europe and America sociologists think in terms of alternative utopias, futurology, coping with future shock, constructing and coping with a cybernetic society, beating the ecological crisis (zero growth rate), the death of God theology, counterculture, consciousness III and the greening of America. None of this has any real kinship or even affinity with the modernization of the under-developed countries of Asia and Africa except in honorific senses. For the West the problem, as the mainstream sociologists see it, is that of continuing progress, of growing to maturity and coping with a new modernity; in a word, of getting through a time of troubles. For us (say, the Indians) modernization implies something akin to religious conversion.

The contemporary theory of modernization is in one important sense a direct continuation of Comtean sociology, in another and profounder sense it represents its definitive failure. Comte believed that the scientific-industrial form of society that was replacing the ancien régime in Europe would be the ultimate form of the future world society. He thought that this form of social order, on the strength of its indisputable intrinsic superiority, would eventually be adopted universally; there would be no need for wars or other coercive methods, and precisely for this reason the new science of society had to be invented and established to preside over the universal diffusion of scientific-industrial society. Modernization theory also aims at this very diffusion in the non-Western world and hence it may be seen as the continuation of Comtean universalism. At the same time, however, it represents its manifest failure because: (i) there have been two world wars within less than a century of Comte's death, thus falsifying a major thesis of Comtean sociology that industrial society makes war an anachronism; (ii) in the Western world itself there have emerged two forms of 'universal' scientific-industrial society (the Comtean and the Marxist) which, whether or not they are based on common fundamental postulates, regard themselves as fundamentally opposed to each other; (iii) even a century after Comte the scientific-industrial society has not been globally realized: large parts of Asia, Africa and Latin America are far from having attained the full level of industrialization; and (iv) in the Western world itself, the scientific-industrial society which Comte implicitly absolutized has become completely obsolete.

This sociology of modernization is of course incompatible with Marxism. Marxian universalism is futuristic, but in a different sense. For Comte, it was a question of the progressive universal diffusion of an emergent form of society that had already appeared, while for Marx, the social form that ought to be universalized had yet to arrive. The Marxian equivalent of the theory of modernization is, therefore, the praxiology of world-wide socialist revolution. But this theory has its own fundamental contradiction today. Because of a world-wide diffusion (violent and non-violent) of the theory and practice of socialist revolution, which were historically wholly the product of European history, the superstructures tend to be revolutionized in non-Western countries long before the productive forces and productive relations come to be correspondingly revolutionized. Conversely, because of the availability of all kinds of technology, productive forces can be changed in a major way without any corresponding revolution in the social structure. This means that the necessary relation between superstructure and infrastructure posited in Marxism no longer holds. Second, the contradiction inherent in nuclear technology (whether for war, peace or industry) and in unlimited industrial growth, which makes world peace and the survival of mankind extremely precarious, has no resolution in the Marxian dialectic. The ecological crisis and the constant threat of a nuclear holocaust cannot be coped with in terms of the prospects for the coming global triumph of Marxism. For there can still be major conflicts between different nations all accepting Marxism-Leninism.

Why does the whole world cling to the theory of modernization and to the Marxist theory of socialist revolution, both of which are utterly untenable and riddled with irredeemable inconsistencies? The idea of modernization of the non-Western people, the idea of a socialist revolution for world communism, and the idea of a scientific-industrial form of life which is common to both, are the latest forms of the universalist spirit of European civilization. They succeed the Imperial Idea (Roman Empire), the Christian Idea (Christendom, world Christianity), and the idea of the White man's Burden (the British Empire). Against this background, we should consider two different but converging models that represent the view of the liberal or non-Marxist West. One is that of Gellner: 'If a doctrine conflicts with the acceptance of the superiority of the scientific-industrial societies over others, then it really is out'.[25] Gellner offers the following reasons for this: (i) modern science and its application have absolute and manifest cognitive and technical superiority over all other scientific and technological systems known to man; (ii) this superiority provides a tremendous advantage in respect of social, economic and political power, and also in respect of the satisfaction of needs; (iii) the acceptance of this superiority is the only way in which the problem of historical and cultural relativism can be solved.

The other model is represented by Parsons and Bellah. In their different ways they try to show that the uniqueness and superiority of American 'scientific industrial' societies over all other past and contemporary societies is unquestionable because the analytic evolutionary history of mankind offers overwhelming evidence in its favour.[26] The important difference between the two models is that Gellner's claims to be independent of evolutionism and comparative history: the implicit argument is a sort of reductio ad absurdum. Gellner's model, which is the more profound one, presupposes that absolute criteria are available for judging the cognitive superiority among different systems of knowledge, whether synchronically or diachronically; and in a history-conscious society such as the scientific-industrial, the diachronic perspective is always implicitly present. But the propriety of such a presupposition is precisely what constitutes the problem of historical relativism.

None of these models will stand logical scrutiny. What matters at this level of thought is not facts and their analysis, but insight. And it is Husserl who speaks with an authentic voice, not Gellner, the despair of whose acute and sophisticated analyses, like those of Goffman at a different level, is muted by his ironical existential stance. But only saints can bear the burden of irony; not even Kierkegaard could cope with the daimonia implicit in all irony. And so Husserl says:

> The spiritual image – what is it? It is exhibiting the philosophical idea immanent in the history of Europe (of spiritual Europe). To put it another way, it is its immanent teleology, which, if we consider mankind in general, manifests itself as a new human epoch emerging and beginning to grow, the epoch of a humanity that from now on will and can live only in the free fashioning of its being and its historical life out of rational ideas and infinite tasks.[27]

We get here an insight into the real nature of Gellner's asymmetrical solution to the central problem of modern Euro-American civilization, which, in one word, is hubris.

> The three values which seem to me to be immanent in modern civilization are equality, personality and universality. All these are

> perhaps subordinate to the ultimate inspiration of the modern age which I shall call the *Promethean ambition* – the urge, to borrow a Cartesian expression, to become the *masters* and *possessors* of nature.[28]

The same idea in a different form is the principle of the Marxist theory of the coming world socialist revolution. The futuristic, eschatogical and gnostic nature of the Marxist school is the source of the tremendous energy that in certain contexts world-communist power seems to possess. This also explains why in some ways (and in specific contexts) Marxism seems to be a sound or inevitable alternative to liberal Western civilization. But this very gnostic futurism also makes it more difficult for Marxism (Communism, Leninism, Maoism etc.) to be self-critical and see its telos of universal domination as hubris.

VII

In the course of this critical survey of the development of sociology, the relation of history and science has come up again and again; and it is time now to examine it on the general theoretical level. The entire modern Western social science is built up on the following postulates:

1. No absolute transcendental principle is to be acknowledged.
2. The new universalism is to be founded on history and science ('The two muses of the modern age', said Flaubert, 'are history and science').
3. There is and ought to be perpetual growth and novelty.
4. The modern age is absolute, unprecedented, unsurpassable, universal and eternal.

History is the crux. Not only is it the dividing line between tradition and modernity, but also the central point of many contemporary theoretical divisions; between Lévi-Strauss and Sartre, and from a certain point of view, between non-Marxist and Marxist sociology, between Chomsky and Skinner, between microsociology and macrosociology.

The difficult (indeed, insoluble) question of the relation between eternity and time (history) is by no means new or modern; it is as old as human thought. What is uniquely modern is the use of the idea of history in a non-relative manner; that is, as a concept that is fully meaningful and yet is not paired with any other concept by way of contrast or kinship. As our survey of sociology shows, the entire energy of modern thinking is bent upon one task, to free man from eternity; for modern thought rejects the idea that history cannot be meaningful except in terms of transtemporal (trans-historical) telos. The historical order is contingent. Looking at any given constellation of past events, reflecting on a specific course that the history of a given people took, one finds that there could have been an entirely different constellation of events, history could have taken a different course. If this is true, contingency rules the domain of human history; indeed, it rules human life itself.

Let us note two major problems of the contingency of history: first, the problem of the ground of meaning and value in the human realm, and second, the problem of man's freedom. If history is the realm of contingency, in which neither meaning and values nor law and freedom are conceivable, how is it that the modern age seeks to found them exclusively in history, rejecting almost violently their age-old foundations? Man's experience of history, his historicity, his faith in history, derive essentially from an experience of uprooting. This uprootedness is expressed in three basic forms, conversion, conquest, and colonisation, which may go together but are independent of each other.

It is not suggested that the experience of temporality, contingency and historicity begins with the modern age. Traditional man was no less aware of temporality, contingency and history. What distinguishes so sharply modern Western man's experience of history as a problem is the faith in the autonomy of history. Traditional man experiences temporal life and contingency, and hence history, not as a problem but as a mystery, and he transcends the contingency of history by myth and metaphysics. It is the urge to do away with traditional myth and metaphysics and to solve the problem of historical relativism by history itself which defines the task the modern age sets for itself.

Since it is the twin gods of the modern age – history and science – who preside over sociology, its present crisis is rooted in their complicated relationship. I have argued that the divinization of history is not essentially a consequence of the rise of modern science. On the other hand, the historical and the scientific consciousness which together form the fundamental character of modern Western man are independent of, and ultimately incompatible with, each other.

When Western man's faith in his tradition began to decay he naturally questioned the idea of transcendence and attempted to abolish it. The dialectical-logical impossibility of any such attempt led to his discovery of time and history. Having given up the traditional understanding of time and history in terms of myth, metaphysics and theology, he now requires a new principle, namely Vico's: one can understand only that which one can make. This principle was accepted not only for history but also for science, with the most far-reaching consequences. In the realm of history the principle means that either history is made by man or he cannot really understand it. In the same way, in the natural-scientific domain it means: either nature is eventually remade by man or he cannot fully understand it. We should also note that this principle in its very formulation implies a goal and a criterion of genuine understanding; namely, the power of creating and recreating the object one wants to understand.

The paradigm for the working of this principle is well-known: the scientific study and understanding of nature gives man, through technology, the power to conquer and control nature for his own purposes. In the same way, the scientific study of man and history will give him (through planning, social control, social engineering?) the power to be master of his own history. This idea is fundamental to all social science, and to most modern social philosophy and philosophical sociology. But let us first examine the notion of the mastery of nature. The fact is that modern man's technology starts any number of irreversible processes, some of which have far-reaching consequences that he would like to avoid and hence seeks to eliminate or minimise, but so far without success. Worse still, there are many consequences which are not anticipated. In view of this, it is nonsense, in this context, to speak of the 'conquest of nature', for here man is creating new fatalities for himself, and this is neither conquest nor direction of either history or nature.

All this, of course, is now an utter commonplace. But our point is that it is still not realized that the trouble with us is not that we have overshot our targets, but that we have been shooting in the dark. It is the telos of man's history that alone can give meaning to science and technology, and not the other way round. The neglect of this normal relation between history and technology has brought us to the absurd situation where our history becomes a slave to something whose meaning we don't understand. It is sometimes argued that 'modern' science and technology are the expressions of 'modern' Western man's Promethean spirit. If we follow this line of thinking, we have to consider the fact that since no meaning can be attached to the notion of conquering or manipulating nature, except in terms of a given philosophy of history, the meaning of this Promethean spirit must be examined in the context of human history; that is, it must primarily mean mastery of history. What then do we mean by the mastery of history?

That we should understand this notion on the analogy of scientific, technological control of nature is as deep-rooted in sociology today as it is completely untenable. If, following our analysis, it is accepted that the notion of mastery of nature acquires its meaning in terms of history, then mastery of history evidently cannot be understood by analogy with it. Let us, therefore, consider some other conceptions of the 'mastery of history'. Sociologists talk about planned and directed change, and creative response to the newest technological revolution. Alternatively, they talk of controlling science and technology. The theory of planned or directed change need not detain us, for if our analysis of the meaning of mastery of history is valid, this theory can only be a disguise for a theory of public relations for the vested interest of certain classes in a given society. The notion of creative response to continuing technological revolution, besides pulling in a somewhat different direction, can amount to nothing more than a justification of the ways of technology to men, with a view to making them happy (blessed) victims of the technological society.

The most widely accepted notion in this context is that of control of science, and especially technology. Before examining it, we will turn to the best-known application of science to history and history to science: evolutionary progress, which in effect constitutes the very climate of modern life. The essence of evolutionary progressivism is that mankind has a linear historical unity, and the overall pattern of human history is steady though uneven, moving consistently in a direction that is on the whole a movement from good to better to best. Evolutionary progressivism is thus, in effect, a philosophy of history; or perhaps the foundation of any modern philosophy of history. But it is logically and historically completely untenable. Leaving aside here the logical objections, let us note that the history on the basis of which the socio-cultural evolutionist theory is possible at all as a philosophy of history, is essentially the history of Europe plus the discovery of primitive peoples who are supposed to be historyless. If all the known historic and prehistoric civilizations are taken into account the evolutionist philosophy of history becomes immediately an embarrassment. And there are many other problems; for example, that of devising a suitable theory of survivals, and the closely related question of the relationship between the so-called primitive peoples and the traditional cultures and civilizations of China, Egypt, Babylon, India, etc.

VIII

Sociology has been the new universalism of our age. This universalism, though in a sense a successor to imperialism and Christendom, differs fundamentally from all previous universalisms. It is not founded on any absolute; it rejects all transcendence; in all spheres it aspires to substitute horizontal for vertical unities; it has a parochial centre, but acknowledges none; it claims to be relativistic and historical but is founded on the absolutization of modern science; it promises to eliminate metaphysics and theology but achieves only their vulgar transpositions and perversions.

Sociology, therefore, is rooted in Christianity; its doctrines, dogmas and history. In one of its most fundamental aspects the crisis of sociology is the crisis of the Christian Mission. My argument in this essay has been to show that so far sociology has not been able to 'free' itself from its Christian roots; consequently it suffers from an internal contradiction, a schism in the soul. Christianity (like all religion) is founded on a mystery: the mystery of Jesus Christ: Jesus who was Christ; the Incarnation which takes place really in time and is yet wholly and absolutely beyond time. This paradox, this major mystery, this *skandalon* is firmly acknowledged in Christian theology; if you cannot accept this, Christianity cannot be meaningful for you. As the successor to Christian theology, sociology too is founded on a central paradox; namely, the advent of modern science. This event occurs in history, it is involved in all the contingencies of the historical realm, it partakes of all the infirmities and glories of the human mind; and yet it is unique, absolute, universal, outside all history, above all relative values, beyond all time. This paradox, this plain contradiction, this major 'scientific mystery', this *skandalon* is not acknowledged in sociology. Even so, if you do not accept this, you cannot be even a modern man, to say nothing of being a sociologist. The crucial difference – staggering for a non-Westerner in whom somehow, providentially, some intelligence and a little human dignity survive – is that while the Christian is asked to accept something that is acknowledged as contradiction, the student of sociology, the aspirant to modernity, is required to accept an unacknowledged contradiction not in the name of mystery or faith but in the name of reason and science.

Christian theology is centred in the Christian Revelation: and this Revelation is about man, nature, cosmos and God. Sociology is centred in modern scientific knowledge which is about nature alone. This is the second major contradiction of sociology: the advent of the science and technology which sociology celebrates, and of which sociologists are the missionaries, should, from the prevailing social science viewpoint, be seen as an event in the realm of nature. Science and technology give man knowledge about nature and power over its processes, not knowledge about man and power over his history. And yet the sociologist must take science (scientific knowledge about nature) as the paradigm of man's knowledge of himself and history; he must accept technology (the new man-nature relationship governed by science) as the absolute paradigm for all human relationships as well as for man's relationship to history. In other words the sociologist has the task of translating the nature and destiny of nature as revealed by science into the nature and destiny of man. This has, perhaps, a faint parallel in Christian theology. At one time the theologians had the task of assimilating Greek philosophy – more precisely the Aristotelian system – into the Christian Theology. But the sociologist's task is, of course, much harder: for, unlike Christian theology and Greek philosophy which have God and Cosmos and Man in common, there is nothing in common between sociology and ('modern' physical) science, except negatively, the rejection of God and transcendence. True, sociology too posits the unity of man and nature and hence there is social science as the human-historical arm of ('modern' physical) science just as the State was the temporal arm of the Church at one time; there is unified science and the projected 'only one science' mutually inclusive of man and nature (Marx). But the marvel is that the sociologist who has already rejected the transcendental and cosmological unity of nature and man in God should now want to bridge the consequent chasm between the two on the basis of the same science which, in the first place, created it. In other words, he must have faith in Science as both the supreme Destroyer and the ultimate Redeemer.

Having arisen as the new saviour of man for whom God is dead, the inner ambition of sociology is to replace the cosmological consciousness of man by the evolutionary-historical consciousness; and Science obviously is the Redeemer of History, for it is the new God in whose name the transcendental mythical-cosmological consciousness has been rejected. And yet, the historical and the scientific consciousnesses are incommensurable; hence the deepest urge of science is to abolish history. Sociology is possible if and only if it is possible and desirable to achieve the full conversion of history into technology, of doing into making, of action into event. We are now at a juncture when this decision can be temporized no longer.

The new universalism represented by sociology has been based on an unredeemed and unredeemable promise; and hence sociology has been the bearer of a false consciousness for Western man. Being rooted in Christianity and its history, it has had a profound meaning for Western culture. What, however, is the meaning of sociology (or of the social sciences in general) for people in whose history Christianity can, in no way, be said to be central? What does the acceptance of sociology by Asians and Africans signify? The universality of sociology? Or, the wretchedness of, say, Indians?

The redemption of sociology and of 'modern' man lies not in reflexive, critical or dialectical sociology, nor in black or Chinese or Indian sociologies. An intellectual revolution is required so that the evolutionary mode of thought yields place to cosmological thinking, autological perspective is established in place of the anthropological. This calls for *metanoia.* No less. May one hope for it?

NOTES

[1] Usually sociology is broadly defined as the science of society, not of man *and* society nor even of man *in* society (the latter in fact is often used to define anthropology). Such a definition really leaves out man from the scope of sociology in any but a non-essential, peripheral way and this remains true even when we remember that society in this context means human society. This thesis cannot be argued here at any length but the main argument is that the category society is defined in sociology *principally* as an aggregate; that is why it has been until very recently customary to include a discussion of animal society in sociology textbooks and the idea persists in the hyphenated concept of mass-society. An aggregate whose members are humans is then defined as human society with the proviso that it possess certain further characteristics. For instance, the possession of a symbol is often postulated as an indispensable and specific characteristic of human society. Now this can be regarded as human character if and only if it is not insisted, as sociology does, that we must ultimately develop a sociological theory of symbolism. Our phrase 'man and society' is an attempt to suggest the fundamental dilemma of a non-metaphysical, non-cosmological sociology which in the last analysis cannot define itself either in terms of man or in terms of society.

[2] Most histories of social thought would, however, disagree with any such view. Historians of social thought like to survey its development from lore to science; at any rate from Plato to Parsons. But this strange denial of both logical and substantive discontinuities between, say Platonic or Thomistic social thought on the one hand, and Comtean, Marxian or Parsonian sociologies on the other, is based on an evolutionary universalism which itself is supported by the postulated continuity in the history of ideas from lore to science. (The kind of

discontinuous history of ideas to which Michel Faucault refers citing the recent work of Bachelard, Canguilhem, Serres and Guéroult has yet to inform the history of social thought. See M. Foucault: *The Archaeology of Knowledge* (London, Tavistock Publications, 1972), Introduction.

[3] It is true that in his *New Science* G. B. Vico recognised God and enunciated a modified cyclic theory, thus clearly accepting filiation with Christian and Greek Traditions. In my view, however, more significant is his thesis that man can understand history or civil society because he makes it; and this thesis is fundamentally anti-Christian and un-Greek. This is what is 'new' in his science.

[4] Henri de Lubac: *The Drama of Atheist Humanism* tr. Edith M. Biby, Cleveland and New York: World Publishing Company, iv. [First edn. 1950].

[5] Auguste Comte: *Discourse sur l'espirit positif* (Paris, 1844), 43. Quoted by Herbert Marcuse, *Reason and Revolution* (Boston, 1960), 353. [First edn. 1941].

[6] Maurice Mandelbaum: *The Problem of Historical Knowledge* (New York: Liveright 1938), 274. Mandelbaum quotes William Stern for an alternative formulation of historical pluralism: 'The total structure of history is to be understood as vertically stratified, not as a single linear connection of occurences [Universal History] and also not as a set of independent historical unitary entities standing side by side [Cultural morphology]. *Op. cit.,* 287.

Michel Foucault's reference to the new historiography in terms of 'discontinuities, systems and transformations, series and threshholds' (*The Archaeology of Knowledge,* op. cit., 13) may be regarded as one of the most recent formulations of historical pluralism.

[7] Ludwig Wittgenstein, *Philosophical Investigations* (Oxford: Basil Blackwell, 1953), 109.

[8] Merton's plea for theories of middle range, the sociologies of Goffman and Oscar Lewis, the argument for literary sociology (Pelz, *The Scope of Understanding in Sociology,* London, Routledge and Kegan Paul, 1974, 237ff, Appendix and passim) are all variations on the anti-universalist theme, each in its own way failing to fulfil its programmatic principle and promise. One of the latest and most sophisticated variations is perhaps Foucault's concept of an archaeology of Knowledge.

[9] In Montesquieu, a most important precursor of social thought,

there is a complicated interplay of universalism and analytical descriptivism. Raymond Aron sums up the position as follows: 'It is perfectly true that there are to be found in Montesquieu statements inspired by the Philosophy of a rational and universal order alongside statements which emphasise the diversity of historical collectivities. But it is not so certain that Montesquieu's thought must be regarded as a clumsy compromise between these two inspirations, as a stage in the gradual discovery of pure "historicity". It can also be seen as a legitimate if imperfect attempt to combine two ways of thinking, neither of which can be entirely eliminated from the exercised human reason'. (Raymond Aron, *Main Currents in Sociological Thought,* Vol. I, Garden City, New York: Doubleday Anchor Books 1968, 58.)

[10] Aron, *op. cit.,* 114.

[11] Humanism was proclaimed by Comte in 1847. A year later he founded the Positivist Society. On 22 April 1851 Comte wrote to Monsieur de Thoulouze: 'I am convinced that I will preach Positivism as the only real and complete religion at Notre-Dame before 1860'. (Quoted in Aron, *op. cit.,* 127).

[12] *Cours de philosophie positive,* Vol. IV, 340-42, quoted in Aron, *op. cit.,* 136.

[13] *Systéme de politique positive,* Vol. II, 2.

[14] See Lubac, op. cit., 132-35.

[15] Karl Marx and F. Engels., *The German Ideology,* ed. R. Pascal (New York: International Publishers, 1947).

[16] Henri Lefebvre, *The Sociology of Marx* (London: Allen Lane the Penguin Press, 1968), 18.

[17] Karl Marx, *Capital,* Vol. I (Moscow: Foreign Language Publishing House, 1954), 117.

[18] David McLellan, ed., *Marx's Grundrisse* (London, Macmillan, 1971), 119-20.

[19] T. B. Bottomore and M. Rubel, *Karl Marx, Selected Writings in Sociology and Social Philosophy* (New York: McGraw-Hill, 1964), 28.

[20] For a discussion of this dictum from *Capital* (Vol. I, Modern Library edition, 201-5), see Hannah Arendt *The Human Condition* (Garden City, New York: Doubleday Anchor Books, 1959), 330, and Chapter III.

[21] One may mention Ethnomethodology (Garfinkel), Cognitive Sociology (Cicourel), Meaning Sociology (John B. Malley), Reflexive Sociology, New Sociology, Radical Sociology, etc. Also there has been

renewed interest in the Dialectical Sociology of the Frankfurt School. Another point to be noted here is that there is considerable overlap between substantive and methodological concerns of recent sociologies and the distinction made here between the two has only a limited value.

[22] Ernest Gellner, *Cause and Meaning in the Social Sciences* (London: Routledge and Kegan Paul, 1973).

[23] Ibid.

[24] Ernest Gellner, *Thought and Change* (Chicago: University of Chicago Press, 1965), 3-5.

[25] Ernest Gellner, *Cause and Meaning in the Social Sciences,* op. cit., 72.

[26] R. N. Bellah, 'Civil Religion in America', *Deadalus* Vol. 96, No. 1, 18.

[27] Edmund Husserl, *Phenomonology and the Crisis of Philosophy,* Tr. by Quertin Lauer. (New York: Harper Torchbooks, 1965), 156.

[28] Raymond Aron, *Progress and Dissillusion,* (Harmondsworth: Penguin Books, Ltd.), 305.

6

EMPIRICAL KNOWLEDGE AND SOCIAL VALUES IN THE CUMULATIVE DEVELOPMENT OF SOCIOLOGY

Stefan Nowak
University of Warsaw

I. SYMPTOMS OF CRISIS IN SOCIOLOGY

The task of our Symposium is to answer the question whether there is a crisis in sociology. I think the fact that such a question has been asked at an international meeting of sociologists constitutes at least a partial answer to it. It implies that there are a sufficient number of sociologists who *feel* that their discipline might be in a critical situation. Before trying to answer the question directly, let us consider what kind of crisis they might have in mind, because a crisis in a science may mean any of at least three different things:

1. First, it can mean that the given science cannot develop or even

Paper prepared for the Round Table 'Is There a Crisis in Sociology?' at the VIIIth Congress of Sociology, Toronto, August 1974. The present extended and modified version of this paper was written during the author's fellowship at the Center for Advanced Study in the Behavioral Sciences at Stanford, California.

cannot exist in a certain set of social conditions, because *these conditions do not, in the most simple and external sense, permit it to do so.* The means used can range from the pressure of public opinion not to develop it, through denial of the economic means necessary to the science, to simply bureaucratic decision blocking the development of the science as a whole or in certain essential sub-areas.

2. Second, it can mean that the science, developing more or less 'correctly' from the point of view of certain internal standards, *does not fulfill some of its external social functions* in the way it should according to certain normative standards of its social functions. In such case we may be inclined to blame the situation on either the society for not using the science in the 'proper' way, or the scientists themselves for developing their discipline in such a way that it is of little social relevance.

3. Finally, it can mean that the *crisis lies in the science itself.* Sometimes this may be a temporary phenomenon, as for example when the old 'paradigms' which were providing the guiding principles for the development of the science do not work any longer, and the science has not yet been able to develop a new workable paradigm. In some other cases the crisis is of a more profound character, as when the representatives of the given science cannot agree on the basic assumptions of their discipline, its nature and goals, and this disagreement is not solved for quite a long period.

There is no doubt that in some countries we have definitely a crisis of the first kind, and one of the papers in our Symposium discusses a typical case of this category.[1] There is also no doubt that there are various symptoms of crisis in sociology with respect to its social functions. According to some writers[2] contemporary sociology is performing the wrong social functions, being committed to conservative social values. In saying this they usually have in mind ideological functions of certain findings and theories, their real or possible impact upon human values and attitudes on a mass scale, as factors strengthening or legitimizing various

Establishments. But one can question as well the more practical, instrumental functions of contemporary sociology, the purposes for which it is being 'used' by different groups and agencies which need sociological information for guidance in their practical actions. These uses can also be judged from the standpoint of specific normative standards, and we might ask the question: Who is applying these social findings and theories and for what purposes, and what are the possible or actual instrumental social consequences of the various sociological orientations, i.e. what are their most likely practical uses?

But the question of the instrumental uses of sociology can be asked in more general terms: What are the *possibilities* of contemporary sociology in the area of guiding social actions, *to what degree is it really prepared to transform reality in a scientifically justified way?* In order to see this problem more clearly let us imagine a kind of mental experiment. Suppose there is a society which constitutes an ideal from the point of view of a sociologist's dream. It is guided by social values which sociologists accept (here we would have to assume a certain uniformity of values among sociologists) and it is eager to follow practical recommendations formulated by sociologists, transforming them into practical social actions. Now let us ask ourselves honestly: How much would we have to offer this society on the basis of our findings and theories, and especially *to what degree would we be able to agree on such recommendations* derived from our theoretical and diagnostic knowledge? The answer is – unfortunately – not too favorable to sociology, and one can easily predict that the number of recommendations for the solution of one specific social problem would not be much smaller than the number of sociologists involved.

If this is a correct prediction, then we have to assume that our discipline is also in a state of internal crisis. We could say, of course, that this means only that our discipline and especially our social theories have not been developed sufficiently to allow social scientists to make correct predictions and therefore to formulate scientifically valid rules of social action on which all are able to agree. This would entail admitting we are now at the stage of development medicine was before Pasteur, when every doctor was a representative of a specific 'school' and on the basis of the theory of his school along with certain practical experiences he made his recommendations to patients. This is probably to some degree true, but I believe the situation is much more serious than a mere stage of development, and that contemporary sociology is in a state of profound crisis which has its roots in the philosophical foundations of our discipline.

As we know, some critics of sociology have not limited their criticisms to 'unmasking' the conservative functions of particular social theories or approaches. They have attacked the very idea that sociology might be a science at all in the normal sense of the term. What do I mean by a normal science? I mean by this a discipline in which a certain amount of intersubjective agreement is possible with respect to both its findings and its theories. I mean a discipline in which these findings are subject to a cumulative growth, in which the propositions established by one generation of researchers are modified or even rejected by others who on the basis of certain special features: the cumulativeness is usually limited tion is right, in such a way that it would be accepted by a majority of other researchers. In general I mean a discipline which develops according to certain standards accepted by all those working in it, and in which we observe the process of its cumulative development.

It would not be fair to say that the process of cumulative

development does not exist in our science at all; it is quite visible in some areas of sociology. But in sociology it has certain special features: The cumulativeness is usually limited to those scientists who are working within the same paradigm, or as we used to say, who accept the same approach to study of social phenomena. One of the basic features of sociology is that each of the approaches seems to have a dynamics of its own. Even if there are really paradigms in any sense of this highly ambiguous term, they lack the basic feature of the paradigm, i.e. they do not with the passage of time replace one another in a way that would obtain the general acceptance of all concerned. The rise, development and disappearance of different approaches which we can observe in both the recent and the more distant history of our discipline has very little in common with the appearances of new paradigms in the natural sciences, where the new paradigms become necessary when the old ones cannot account for newly emerging facts and theories. The occurrence and disappearance of paradigms in sociology seems to have much more in common with changes in women's fashions – which can hardly be accepted as a satisfactory situation in science.

Moreover, this situation has been defined by some as a normal, not to say a desirable one. Predep Bandyopadhyay in his excellent criticism of 'radical methodology' presented this view in the following way:

> Disagreements among sociologists are in principle irreducible, since they involve different paradigms, evaluative statements and different purposes . . . . Value neutrality and objectivity are both unattainable . . . . Therefore, there are and will be several sociologies, none of which are objectively true but merely different ways of looking at society, and – in the words of a fashionable school in sociology – different ways of constructing social reality.[3]

If one could say that all these attacks were merely the misunderstandings of outsiders who, due to lack of competence in the philosophy of science, had misinterpreted some rather banal statements about the relations between social sciences and societies, there would be no reason to state the existence of an internal crisis of sociology. One is not necessarily responsible for the errors of one's incompetent critics. But unfortunately this has not been the case with sociology. Most of the arguments by which the scientific status of sociology has been questioned have come from academic sociology. In some cases these arguments were presented as a caricature and reflected certain views which could be found in a more balanced and at least partially acceptable form in sociology itself. In other cases no caricatured exaggeration was necessary.

Therefore I would like in this paper to discuss certain problems pertaining primarily to the existence of different schools in sociology, and such related problems as 'objectivity' and 'value involvement', because in my opinion lack of agreement on these problems constitutes the basic obstacle in the cumulative development of our discipline, and therefore might be identified as a basic source of its internal crisis. The problem of the theoretical consequences of value involvement deserves special consideration because the radicals have attacked the methodological assumptions of traditional sociology in the name of certain social values: equality, freedom and human dignity. But many sociologists share these values with their critics, and it is perhaps for this reason that rebuttals have not been freely forthcoming. Thus polemics revealing the spurious relationship between radical social values and radical methodology have been rather rare.[4]

However, these problems are related to crisis in the first and second senses as well: wrong notions about the relations between sociology and society, about its functions for the society, create expectations which sociology can never – at least as a scientific discipline – satisfy. At the same time, by contributing to the internal crisis in our discipline such notions indirectly diminish the possible applications of sociology to the transformation of society in the direction corresponding to our value systems. Moreover, we should also remember that any element of internal crisis in sociology, and especially those arguments which question the possibility of its existence as a normal science, may be used as an argument against sociology by social forces which, from the point of view of their interests, perceive the existence of sociology as dangerous or at least inconvenient. Therefore, those for whom crisis in the first sense distinguished above is of primary importance should remember that the elimination of internal crisis from sociology may be relevant in this respect as well.

In general, I agree with Franco Ferrarotti that it is 'important to rediscover the nature of the sociological enterprise, its necessarily unfinished character, its problematic disposition and its ambiguity',[5] provided the main goal of rediscovery and reassessment of the sociological enterprise will be accompanied by the elimination of ambiguities, wherever this is possible. The present paper is an attempt in that direction.

II. CUMULATIVE CHARACTER OF EMPIRICALLY TESTED PROPOSITIONS AND THEORIES

When speaking about the possibility of cumulative development in sociology it seems reasonable to start by looking for areas in which an unquestionable agreement can be reached. It seems that the easiest thing to agree on is the truth of certain propositions.

Let us say that a proposition is true when the facts really are as it states. In empirical sciences it is more convenient to say that a proposition is empirically justified to the degree that we are entitled – on the basis of certain data – to assert with greater or smaller probability its full or approximate truth. Now, without going much into a philosophical discussion of the meaning of the term 'empirical proposition' (some of these problems will, nevertheless, have to be mentioned below), let us say that any two sociologists should be able to agree on the empirical validity of such statements as 'New York City has a given number of inhabitants'. They should also be able to agree on the truth of the statement that in a certain sample of persons studied by a social mobility researcher, those subjects whose parents belonged to the lowest paid group have the smallest probability of getting into highly paid occupations or of finishing university studies.

One can also say that most sociologists should be able to agree on some generalizations from such observational data, even if the intended validity of thc conclusions overreaches the extent of the observed reality, especially if the chance of inductive errors in generalizing procedures can be more or less rigorously estimated. This can be done most easily where the studied population constitutes a random sample of the larger population, because in such situations the rules of statistical inference define the probability of making errors of different size, but we could expect a certain amount of agreement also in less standardized research situations. Thus, e.g., most sociologists would probably agree that the amount of social inequality in contemporary Sweden is smaller than in contemporary France, or (even without too rigorous data) that the amount of illiteracy in Africa is much larger than in Europe. In other situations, where the risk of inductive error cannot be so easily estimated, different scientists may differ in their belief as to the empirical validity of certain generalizations, but at least they should agree that their empirical validity may be questioned.

Nothing is changed when these propositions (especially the empirically validated generalizations) are related to each other in such a way that we would be inclined to call them 'theories'. The term theory is used in many different ways and there is not enough space in this paper to mention all of them. The meaning to which I would like to subscribe defines theory as a set or system of empirically testable general laws or law-like statements which can be used for the explanation and/or prediction of the phenomena within the realm of their applicability.

The theory is therefore not identical with certain problem orientations, although the kinds of problems of interest to a scientist may co-determine the theory he will formulate and the theory will be composed of hypothetical solutions to these problems. Nor are concepts identical with theories. Concepts constitute a better or worse language in which we might eventually formulate a theory. Proper conceptual language determines to a high degree the value of a theory, but it does not replace it. What is clear is: We should choose such concepts as will be most useful on the most general scale; i.e. with the use of which we can formulate the best possible laws and their whole systems.

There is no place in this paper for reviewing the characteristics of good theoretical concepts; their optimal shape depends upon the nature of the phenomena studied, and on the kind of questions to which the theory should constitute an answer. We can say, e.g. that if they are classificatory concepts denoting certain sub-areas of reality, they should denote classes of phenomena whereby one can formulate a relatively large number of true, i.e. testable and tested, and at the same time possibly general, propositions. If they refer to more abstract properties or dimensions, they should be defined so that they can occur in the same meaning in many different theoretical propositions, etc. What is more important is that having these criteria (and many others omitted here) in mind, one can rationally argue which of two (or more) proposed sets of concepts is better for the formulation of the theory in question.

The elementary requirement of any theory is that the hypotheses, once they have been conceptualized, are (directly or indirectly) empirically testable by the theory's consequences. Therefore, all that has been said regarding testability – and consequently about the possibility of getting inter-subjective agreement on the truth, plausibility, and finally the hypothetical character of propositions – applies in the same degree to theories, if they are understood in the propositional sense.

However, all tested theories are at least potentially cumulative. Each of them constitues a contribution to the totality of social knowledge quite independently of the value assumptions or approaches which led to the formulation of the research problems to which the theory constitutes the answer. Cumulativeness means also that each such previously tested theory (as we know, the verification of a universal proposition is never complete) may be rejected or modified by new empirical evidence. Its conceptualization may be challenged by demonstrating that reformulating its propositions with the use of other concepts will increase the generality of the theory or its explanatory or predictive power. And this is again independent of any value judgments or prior assumptions. Such theories may be cumulative in a more general sense as well, inasmuch as they can sometimes be meaningfully related to each other. By relating different theories to each other (or by finding that they are apparently unrelated, at least at the given stage of our knowledge) we obtain a more and more comprehensive structure of theoretical knowledge about social phenomena.

Here one should mention one problem, namely, the old dream of systematizing all relevant theoretical knowledge about society into one unique and all-inclusive theory. In sociology this dream takes usually one of two forms. The first starts from reductionist assumptions and the attempt is made to construct a general behavioral theory from which all other social theories can be derived. The other approach to realizing the dream starts from the other end and aims to construct a theory of macrosociological type. Both approaches to an all-inclusive theory tend to end with declarations that they eventually will unify all sociological theories. But unfortunately no theory can be simply declared; it has to be formulated and tested, and the same applies to an all-inclusive social theory.

The dream that there will be one theory for one science does not seem to be justified by the development of most of the sciences, when we study them historically. This does not mean we should not work toward a continual integration of our theories by building more and more comprehensive theoretical structures, of either a reductive[6] or a systemic type. But we have also to assume that whatever our progress in this direction we will have to live for a long time with many partial theories – mutually complementary, and cumulative in different senses of the term, applicable for different aspects of social reality, answering to different theoretical questions, and useful for different practical social purposes.

In saying that different theories can be potentially cumulative, I do not mean to say that all theories we may find in contemporary (or classical) sociology constitute empirically valid systems of generalizations formulated with the use of optimal sets of concepts, and therefore that they should be included in their present form. I am of quite the opposite opinion. I think they are often badly formulated and poorly conceptualized, and their empirical evidence is of questionable value. What I want to say is only that we should work on the improvement of those theories and criticize them in the way one does in any other science, i.e. on the basis of relevant empirical evidence and not by revealing their usually 'spurious contradiction' to our own 'theoretical approach'.

III. EMPIRICAL AND NORMATIVE COMPONENTS IN THE DIVERGENT INTERPRETATION OF FINDINGS

Certainly not all the differences of opinion and divergent interpretations of the same data in sociology have a spurious character. Let us now look at those where the differences are real in order to see which of them can be solved on an empirical basis or more generally within an area of argumentation which allows resolution in terms of strictly scientific discourse, and which cannot be so solved because they are related to differences in scientists' focus of interests and directly or indirectly to differences in their value systems.

a. The most simple case would be when one theoretician says that a certain general relation exists between two or more variables while the other says that is not true.

In this situation it can be said that at least one of them is wrong and that it is up to empirical studies to demonstrate who is right. Actually what is usually the case in such situations is that both scientists are partially right and partially wrong, because they both omit in their theoretical formulations certain additional conditions which determine whether this relation occurs. In such case both theories require reformulation. Adding these necessary conditions we obtain a more general theory of which the former two are elements, valid for different sets of conditions omitted before.

b. A second kind of situation is when two theories or at least two laws are incompatible because one of them is more general than the other, and it turns out that the more general theory logically implies the falsity of the less general one in spite of our insistence that this less general theory is true.

Here again, one would think that we have to reject at least one of the theories. But sometimes the impression persists that both theories have sufficient empirical support. The only solution in such case is to reformulate one of the theories in such a way as to eliminate the logical contradiction. This we usually do either by adding some modifiers or qualifiers to the more general theory so that these exclude from the limits of its validity the cases described by the less general theory, or by redefining the concepts of the less general theory so that they do not imply it is derivable from the more general one.

c. The third and most interesting case is when two scientists agree on certain empirical generalizations but disagree on which concepts to use and on which theories should be applied for the interpretation of the findings and generalizations.

In this kind of controversy in sociology we can easily distinguish two types, although they often occur jointly. In the first type the scientists, agreeing upon the validity of certain data, disagree in that each would like to use for the description and interpretation of these findings certain terms and concepts which are different primarily in their expressive function i.e. their meanings have different emotional and evaluative components. In the second type two sociologists insist on using different terms, because they want to treat the observed variables as indicators of different theoretical concepts.

It is well known that most of the concepts we use in sociology not only denote something in reality but also express certain emotions we associate with this reality, convey certain evaluations of it. Two terms may be empirically equivalent, but may at the same time convey quite different emotions and evaluations. Thus, someone who has negative feelings about the term 'social class' may readily accept certain empirical findings about his own society if they are described in terms of 'social strata' but will reject them if interpreted as 'class differentiations'. It may happen that a sociologist will reject the notion of 'nationalism' as describing the attitudes of his co-citizens but will readily accept the term 'patriotism' even though the empirical meaning of it would be equivalent. The reason for his resistance is the same as indicated above, the unwillingness to accept a proposition which, although empirically true, conveys emotions which he cannot accept.

Terminological differences which involve only the evaluative components of the concepts used are of minor importance for the cognitive functions of sociology (although they may be of serious importance for the groups whose social or political interests have been threatened by application of a certain evaluative label). As long as extensions of the terms are identical, they are translatable one into another. Even if two statements formulated by two scientists sound different, the users of the corresponding concepts – even though they cannot agree on the evaluative implications – can agree on the empirical, non-evaluative content of factual statements and theoretical generalizations, and these empirical results would constitute a contribution to the cumulative development of sociology.

This will be possible, however, only if the concepts we use in our empirical studies and in the formulation of our theories are defined with such preciseness that we can distinguish the *denotative* (i.e. empirical) from the *expressive* (i.e. evaluative) components of their meaning. Only then will we be able to say which components denote something that exists in social reality and which express our evaluation of this reality. Needless to say, we are rather far from this ideal in many areas of sociological enquiry. Many of our concepts are defined with the use of terms which in themselves are too vague to secure for the given concept a sufficiently precise meaning. In many other cases we have terms lacking any definitions at all, and the correctness of interpretation of the author's findings and theories depends completely upon an assumed community of meanings as between the author and all of his audience. In such a situation the postulate of a clear distinction of the evaluative and non-evaluative components of the meaning of the concepts used cannot of course, be realized.

Here we come to the next point: What constitutes the empirical, denotative components of sociological concepts? Until now I have assumed for simplicity's sake that we are dealing with phenomena the existence or occurrence of which can be assessed by observation only. As we know, things are not so simple in sociology. While there are, of course, certain phenomena of a strictly observational nature – like the number of inhabitants in a city or the sex of a given individual – most of the phenomena we are interested in are of a more or less inferential nature. We know that certain apparently similar behavioral sequences may have quite different meanings for the behaving persons and for those who are interacting with them, and for this reason we would in our analysis classify into separate conceptual categories a fight between two hooligans and a boxing match between two professionals. We also know that two observationally different situations may, due to the similarity of their meanings, belong to the same conceptual category, e.g. as when we classify both the behavior of Wall Street brokers and the behavior of some scientists during an international conference into one conceptual category of 'competitive behavior', even when from a strictly behavioral point of view the two situations are rather different.

When we do this we are not really very different from natural scientists, who also have to postulate the existence of some unobservable entities and to use certain hypothetical constructs which denote them. The science of genctics wouldn't be possible without the assumption that there exists some unobservable property called a gene; without the postulation of such unobservable entities as atoms or elementary particles the construction of physical and chemical theories wouldn't be possible. The whole area of social reality which we can grasp by the method of 'Verstehen'[7] – to use the old term introduced by Dilthey and developed for theoretical use by Weber – is made up of phenomena which are directly unobservable but which exist in human minds and so determine both individual behavior and social interactions and relations. Therefore we have to take them into account in our conceptual apparatus if we want our concepts to represent social reality with sufficient adequacy and to be useful for explanations and predictions. We have to reflect in our concepts both the meanings of individual behaviors and the whole complex configurations of such meanings, which constitute (jointly with their observable counterparts) the structures and cultures of whole societies.

This means that we will have in the conceptual apparatus of sociology: (1) Concepts which are defined in strictly observational terms – like sex, age or number of interacting persons; (2) Concepts which are 'behaviorally open' and defined strictly in the language of the individual or social meanings of the given behavior or situation – such as the concept of 'competitive behavior; (3) Concepts whose contents combine both meanings and observable behaviors – such as 'cooperation of a group of workers in a factory'.

Whatever the character of the concept, it is useless to empirical science until its content has been somehow related to strictly observable phenomena so that we are able to say on the basis of some observable indicators when the phenomena denoted by it exist or occur. This implies that in social sciences (as well as in natural ones) we are dealing with two levels: The level of observable phenomena which we may use in our research as the 'indicators' of our study, and the level of hypothetical, inferential phenomena which also belong to the studied reality but the existence of which are assessed indirectly by inference from the observable ones and under some additional theoretical assumptions which cannot be discussed here in detail.[8] Nevertheless the problem of whether the hypothetical correspondents of the given observable phenomena exist in a given case is solvable within strictly scientific discourse, just as in everyday practice we understand other people's behaviors and the complex social situations we observe or participate in. If we are wrong in our assessments, future study or future personal experience may correct our mistake. A man may incorrectly interpret someone's behavior as friendly, until some future personal experience informs him of his mistake. A doctor may make an incorrect diagnosis of a patient's illness on the basis of observing its first symptoms, but future observation of the progress of the illness or of the patient's reaction to medical treatment is able in many cases to correct the mistake. We should remember that the relation between the 'indicators' and the validity of some survey data in the study of attitudes would be an example in exactly the same way as knowledge of the symptoms of different illnesses in medicine.

Both the phenomena of the observable level and the meaningful components of social reality are usually rather complex syndromes. Thus scientific concepts never reflect them in all their complexity, but have to concentrate upon certain of the aspects or components only. The same syndrome of 'meaningful behavior' may be an example of 'consumer behavior' for one scientist and an example of 'keeping up with the Joneses' for another, if they concentrate their attention on its different aspects. And the indicator of the two corresponding concepts in this situation may be exactly the same; buying a certain expensive object. This does not mean of course that any case of different inferential interpretations of the same behavior is necessarily valid (actually both may be wrong); it means only that the same empirical situation (whether of a strictly observational or of an inferential nature) can often quite justifiably be categorized into different conceptual categories.

Suppose now that in a certain area of social studies the conceptual apparatus has been defined so that the content of the corresponding concepts is clear to us and we are able to distinguish its denotative and evaluative components. Suppose also that two scientists studying the phenomena within this area agree on the validity of certain strictly observable data, but disagree on the theoretical way they should be interpreted – thus their differences are not primarily related to differences in the evaluative components of the concepts. In such case what the scientists are seeking is to interpret the variables they observe as indicators of different concepts. But here we need to distinguish three kinds of situations.

In the first situation both scientists are interested in treating the indicator (I) as indicating a certain variable (V) (on the meaning of which they agree), but one of them believes that the assessment of I indicates V and the other does not. Two survey analysts disagreeing on the frankness of questionnaire answers and therefore on the validity of some survey data in the study of attitudes woule be an example.

For the second situation, suppose two scientists agree that a certain indicator I potentially indicates a complex, meaningful-behavioral syndrome of social reality. Suppose additionally that they agree on the validity of a certain problem formulation – e.g. they would like to explain a certain behavioral pattern by reference to the values and knowledge of the behaving persons, with the indicator I being used for assessing the existence of such a complex syndrome as 'values and knowledge about social reality possessed by a member of the social group, the culture of which is known to the scientists from other sources'. The indicator for the possible explanatory concept is then simple: membership in the given group. But the question of how the indicated concept should be defined for the purpose of the explanation is equivalent to the question: Which of the totality of values and information possessed by the members of the given group are responsible for the explained behavior, and which are in this theoretical context irrelevant? In other words, the issue is: Which of the great number of concepts that might be used for the denotation of the given indicated situation is theoretically fruitful? It may not be easy to solve such a problem, especially if we take into account the actual situation in sociological theory, but in general this is again a category of problems that can be solved within scientific discourse.

Finally, the scientists may agree on the applicability of a given set of indicators for different concepts, and may also agree that for the given problem formulation the given theoretical interpretation of the indicators would be optimal, but still be in disagreement of a more profound nature having to do with the kinds of questions they are interested in. In such case we are at a level where empirical differences are not involved, and the answers given by different scientists are different because they are determined by the scientists' various individual interests.

This kind of disagreement may also occur before the data have been collected. The two scientists may then be inclined to ask different questions, and consequently to use quite different concepts when asking the questions important for them. Usually they also find that these concepts have to be operationalized in different ways, by the use of different indicators. Then, of course, they will not face the situation of divergent interpretations of the same data because their data will be quite different. In any case they will present different pictures of social reality; sometimes these pictures will refer to roughly the same social phenomena, or may even be based upon different interpretations of the same data.

Now it may happen that one scientist will not accept the findings and generalizations of another research as contributions to the development of sociology, not because these are

– in his opinion – false in any of the senses distinguished above, but because he does not view the questions to which these propositions constitute answers as relevant questions of sociology. Differences in understanding as to what constitutes (or better, should constitute) relevant problem areas of sociology produce as many obstacles in the process of its cumulative development as do differences about the empirical validity of answers to these problems.

IV. NORMATIVE AND EMPIRICAL ASSUMPTIONS OF PARTICULAR APPROACHES

Whatever our conclusion on the empirical validity and cumulative nature of particular findings or particular theories, the fact remains that in contemporary sociology these findings and theories can be located in (or rooted in) one of many approaches which exist in our discipline, in one of several schools of sociological thinking. Without trying to define what makes an approach in sociology, we can cite several examples: functionalism, historicism, evolutionism, behaviorism, phenomenology, structuralism – in any of the several meanings of these terms. As I noted earlier, the existence of different approaches as they now stand, and what is much more important the claims of some of them to superiority or unique validity, constitute the basic obstacles in the transformation of sociology into a normal science.

Without entering into a detailed analysis of the content of the various approaches we can say that they may be regarded and compared from several different points of view: What is the particular problem area defined by the particular approach, i.e. what kinds of questions are of special importance for the representatives of the approach? From this standpoint the different approaches are at least potentially complementary, either when they ask quite different questions, the answers to which lead to completely unrelated theories, or when they deal with similar problem areas and lead to related theories.

Once the list (or system) of problems typical for an approach is relatively clear we may ask some other questions, and especially: What are the normative assumptions of the kinds of questions asked – or in other words, what might be the functions of finding the true answers to these questions in the course of scientific investigation?

As we know, when undertaking a certain study we may be motivated by the expectation that the results of the study will have one or more of the following consequences or functions:

1. They may increase, or even basically change, our knowledge about the phenomena in question – let us call this the *cognitive function.*

2. This may lead to transformation of the reality the science is dealing with, by enabling people to find the proper means leading to their goals. What might be called the *instrumental function* of science – or by influencing their world outlooks, attitudes, values and motivations to undertake certain actions, what might be called the *ideological function.*

It should also be noted, however, that even a strictly cognitive function involves a certain value judgment – namely, that one should (or that we as sociologists should) contribute to a better understanding of the mechanisms governing social phenomena, and that this might be sufficient reason to undertake a study. In other words it gives to curiosity the status of a legitimate human value.

The intended functions of or reasons for the undertaking

of a study are not, of course, always identical with the real consequences of the study: someone may have in mind increase of pure knowledge only to have it turn out that as a more or less direct consequence he has contributed to the production of the atomic bomb (as was the case with the theory of relativity) or has changed in an essential way the value systems and world outlook of the whole of mankind (as in the case of Copernicus). In other instances, studies which were undertaken with the aim of realizing strictly instrumental goals have led to discoveries of great cognitive importance (radar being an example). The same holds true in both the natural and the social sciences. Banal as it may be, it must nevertheless be noted that in some discussions of values in sociology, the real consequences of a certain study are often cited as unmasking the value system of its authors or of a representative of an approach. It would seem that we need to distinguish clearly two things: the actual intentions of a scientist when he is formulating a certain research problem, and the actual functions of his work – if we can assess these empirically, or at least the foreseeable possible consequence and uses of his work.

The analysis of the real or foreseeable, possible social consequences of specific social theories or findings is important, not only as an essential part of sociology itself (namely: sociology of sociology) but it is important also on a meta-theoretical level, because:

a) It makes each individual social scientist sensitive to the different kinds of possible functions of his study, permitting him to maximize the intended functions and thus to increase the social or theoretical importance of his research.

b) It produces premises for an inter-subjective agreement on the question of whether with respect to the given set of social values the study of the given problem, or the solution of a certain hypothesis is

> of primary importance, or whether it is desirable at all. Eventually this permits us to distinguish which of the differences in the formulation of our research problems may be 'justified' by the scientist's convictions about the cognitive importance of certain concepts, hypotheses or theories, and which of them explicitly or implicitly reflect differences in value orientations of the scientists and therefore cannot be solved within the area of strictly scientific discourse.

A second category of assumptions is of a different character. These are involved in certain analytic procedures characteristic for the given approach and in certain concepts which are analytically necessary for them. If someone is interested in determining typical patterns of behavior in a certain society, statistics will provide him with a series of alternative but precise ways of understanding what might be 'typical'. If he seeks an estimated risk of error in making his generalizations, the theory of inductive inference constitutes a set of analytic procedures.

The third and the least clear category of assumptions of different approaches understood as some problem areas are the assumptions which refer to some empirical features of the studied reality. The precise formulation of any question about reality actually implies that we assumc something about this reality – only under this assumption asking the given question may make sense. If I ask someone, 'Did you stop beating your wife every morning?' I assume that the person asked did beat his wife before. Otherwise neither the answer 'yes', nor the answer 'no' makes any sense to me.[9]

If we do not study centaurs in contemporary zoology but study elephants, this is because we assume that elephants exist and centaurs do not. If we study the functions of institutions for societies, this is because we assume that the institutions may have some functions for the societies to which they belong. If we study the social causes of institutional change, we must first assume that the institutions do (or at least may) change, and additionally that these changes have or may have social causes. In order to ask: 'Which is the basic factor in the integration of a society, its system of social control or the community of values among its citizens?' I need to have a long list of assumptions which make the formulation of this question sensible. I have to assume that the society is integrated, that it has a system of social control, and that the values of its members are similar; additionally, I have to assume that these two factors are contributing to the integration of the society, and that one of them is the more important one. Only then will a direct answer to the question of such a study make sense.[10]

Such empirical assumptions are sometimes hidden behind certain conceptualizations typical for certain approaches, and they are sometimes implied by the research techniques which characterize some of the approaches. In order to study attitudes, we must assume that the attitudes exist; in order to study them by questionnaire surveys, we have to assume they can be expressed in the form of questionnaire answers, etc. In the case of abstract conceptualizations, the assumption is often reducible to the assertion that the concepts proposed for denoting social phenomena – and the processes and relations among them – are not empirically empty classes. Otherwise it would not make sense to try to study them.[11]

What is important is that as long as these assumptions are of the nature of empirical propositions, one can discuss the problem of their validity and also the problem of the limits of their empirical validity. Since most societies change, it makes sense to study them for answers to the question of what contributes to their change; some societies, however, do not change, at least for certain periods in their history, and then the assumption of the existence of change is not valid for them. Human aggregates may be internally functionalized to various degrees, from a task group working within the strict pattern of division of labor to the amorphic agglomeration of an audience at a theatre performance. The assumptions which make certain theoretical questions sensible for groups or societies of the first kind are not true for the other.

One of the important problems in sociology is the analysis of empirical assumptions of different approaches in order to see to what degree they seem to be justified and what are the empirical limits of their validity. Such an analysis would reveal the empirical legitimacy and limits of applicability of various approaches, as long as they are understood as problem areas.

Different approaches often use different concepts in the study of social reality. These concepts should be evaluated from two standpoints. First, they may be regarded as components of the questions which define the problem area of a particular approach, in which case all that was said above about the validity of empirical assumptions of questions directly applies to the concepts too. But these concepts may occur also in explanatory hypotheses and theories, and in such context we apply to them the criteria of theoretical fruitfulness. If it turns out that two approaches try to answer the same kind of questions, we may legitimately ask which of the proposed sets of explanatory concepts is better for that purpose. The fact that they were proposed by an approach does not make them 'untouchable' in terms of strictly theoretical evaluative standards.

To give an example: In the context of whatever approach leads us to the question of the influence of 'class membership' upon 'attitudes' there is probably only one optimal way of defining for this purpose the concept of 'class' and the concept of 'attitude'; and the final acceptance of a particular conceptualization should be independent of the author's approach and determined only by comparison of the theoretical usefulness of various conceptualizations.

Many approaches include not only certain problems and concepts but also specific theoretical hypotheses and quite developed theories about certain social phenomena, or society in general, its change, etc. Needless to say, each of these theories has to be judged on its own merits, according to normal procedures of empirical verification. And all that has been said about the cumulativeness of theories applies as well to the hypotheses and theories which constitute parts of certain approaches.

Finally, an approach may include a certain set of research procedures, typical operationalization of research variables, and data collection methods – as in the case of, for example, the survey approach, the experimental approach, or the phenomenological approach (with its stress on introspectional data or participant observation).

Now it may be that these indicators define completely for the given approach the content of the corresponding concept, being its operational definitions. In such a case the different approaches would be dealing by definition with different areas of social reality and their findings and generalizations would obviously be unrelated and non-comparable. But, fortunately enough, the period of radical operationalism seems to be over in the methodology of social sciences, and more and more scientists understand that our theoretical concepts should be defined in such a way that the indicators used in the research do not exhaust all their meanings. In some cases they may not even belong to the content of the given concept, as e.g. when we take the 'place of residence' as an indicator of a respondent's 'income'. In such cases different indicators and different research techniques may be regarded as alternative operationalizations of the same theoretical concepts, suitable for different research conditions or for different kinds of populations studied. Then we can of course relate the findings made within different approaches to the same theoretical hypothesis, formulated in a language independent of the different conditional operationalizations of the concepts of the hypothesis. Then we would have for instance, a situation in which the phenomenological analysis of groups or institutions in natural conditions and the sociometric data would lead to independent tests of the same theory of interaction. In any case one should aim toward the direction in which the problems, hypotheses and concepts would determine the research tools, and not the reverse.

Thus we see that from a strictly cognitive point of view the so-called approaches are, at least potentially, complementary. At first they constitute different although often overlapping problem areas, and thus increase the diversity of questions in sociology. Then they formulate different hypotheses aimed toward answering these questions, defining the concepts for the hypotheses and making more or less precise the relations between the phenomena denoted by the concepts. And the hypotheses may be true or false quite independently of which approach was their source, because their truth depends only upon the nature of the reality they refer to. Finally, they may be complementary also in terms of different operationalizations of the same concepts according to the research procedures employed, provided we see clearly that the indicators and techniques which are optimal for one set of conditions are not necessarily optimal for another kind of research situation.

In saying this I do not mean that everything we find in the works of representatives of different schools constitutes a piece of partial truth, and that all we have to do is edit these works, one by one, in a cumulative way and the totality of social knowledge will arise as the sum of these complementary partial views. Quite the contrary. What I propose here is to develop sociology in such direction that the term 'school' will mean the same as it does in any other science: a group of people interested in a common problem area, using similar research techniques and equipment, believing in the hypothetical fruitfulness of certain research hypotheses, and presenting both these hypotheses and the data in support of them for the evaluation of all other scientists, whatever other school they might happen to belong to. From the point of view of this maybe not so distant goal, the existing schools and approaches in sociology constitute only a starting point, and their problems, hypotheses, and research techniques should come to be evaluated from one standard: the degree to which they seem useful for the construction of what might be called an inter-subjectively testable and acceptable body of theoretical knowledge about social phenomena. The first step in that direction would be that the different approaches stop claiming their uniqueness and universal validity, and admit the partial nature of their problem perspectives, concepts, theories, and research techniques, trying at the same time to define that kind of social situations and that kind of research conditions their approach seems to be most suitable for.

V. INSTRUMENTAL FUNCTIONS OF SOCIOLOGY

Let us now look a little more closely at the instrumental functions of sociology, i.e. its applications for the scientifically valid transformation of social reality in the direction prescribed by a certain value system. For this purpose we may use certain more or less descriptive findings of social reality which lead to the diagnosis that some elements or fragments (institutions, patterns of behavior, etc.) do not correspond to normative standards accepted by the scientist or by the group or institution.

Sometimes a correct diagnosis of the state of affairs completes the task of applied social research. This is the case when the means leading to transformation of the reality in the desired direction are more or less obvious. In more complex cases, sociologists may also be asked what should be done in order to eliminate the gap between the reality and that which is normatively postulated. Technically, this means that the sociologist is asked whether in his theoretical knowledge there are any propositions which

a. have as dependent variables conditions that are more or less close to the goals prescribed by the given value system;

b. have as independent variables conditions that could be practically realized by those who postulate these goals or by someone else ready to contribute to their realization;

c. are valid for the situation in which the social action is intended or postulated.

Such theoretical propositions (assuming causal connections between the goals and the means) may or may not already exist in social theory. But if we do not know of a theory (or a more limited generalization) that would satisfy these requirements, then, for purely practical reasons, we would have to develop one. We can therefore say that in many cases the strictly instrumental social application of sociology will have to be accompanied by the development of objective, i.e. true, social theories.

From a strictly instrumental point of view, only empirically valid generalizations and theories have any value at all, because only such theories permit us to make the proper choice of means and therefore to formulate recommendations for practical actions. The same applies to diagnostic studies – if they are not empirically valid they can lead to action that is unnecessary, or to not undertaking action where it would be desirable. Therefore we can say that the instrumental functions of sociology are a powerful factor toward the 'objectivization' of its findings and theories. And, needless to say, the various facts and theories used for the implementation of various societal goals are from a strictly cognitive point of view, cumulative insofar as they are true. This does not mean however, that theories developed for strictly instrumental needs are the same as those developed for more cognitive orientations. A theory is a set of general propositions that can be used for explanations and predictions. But the theories which (due to their generality and level of abstraction) explain a lot are not always the best theories for the purpose of practical prediction in concrete social situations. For this purpose it is often better to have generalizations of limited validity but which within the limits of their validity (e.g. within one society) are able to predict events with great accuracy, than to try to resort to very abstract universally valid general theories. By the same token, generalizations which are of great practical use are not always the best formulation of theories constructed for more cognitive reasons. This is why it is so important that the scientist be cognizant of the reasons for his study.

It is obvious that scientists, since they start their studies from the points of view of diverse value systems, diverse goals, and diverse normative standards will concentrate their attention as well on diverse aspects of their societies when undertaking diagnosis, and on diverse theories needed for the proper choice of means leading to the given set of social goals. Their different pictures of society will be of necessity partial – which does not necessarily mean false – and the different theoretical mechanisms will be complementary, assuming they correctly describe the corresponding causal relations. The real instrumentality of any findings or theories assumes their empirical validity, or simply, their truth.

In general one might say that all social theories, whether they be formulated for cognitive or for practical instrumental reasons may have certain instrumental functions if:

a. the phenomena constituting the dependent variables of the theory are the objects of certain value systems and are positively and negatively evaluated;

b. the phenomena constituting the independent variables of the theory are within the possible range of practical manipulation.

Since almost any phenomenon in the society is likely to be somehow (positively or negatively) evaluated by some groups, the first criterion will eliminate very few theories from having some potential practical applications. But the second criterion imposes limitations, and recognizes significant differences between the groups and institutions in any society; the phenomena which are manipulable by the government or any power elite are not identical with those which might be influenced by the underdogs of the given society. This has nothing to do with objectivity in the sense of the empirical validity of particular theories. But it justifies the assertion that different theories may have different practical social implications.

On the other hand, I believe we usually underestimate the degree of flexibility of possible uses of social theories. Even when the manipulation of a certain variable is limited to one group only, and the manipulation used in the interest of the members of this (let us say, privileged) group, knowledge of the relevant theory may motivate members of other groups toward certain counter-actions. In some cases the simple unmasking of a particular theoretical mechanism may play a positive social function, making its use against the values of the majority practically impossible. Actually it is difficult to find any theory which in different social conditions or milieux could not be applicable for the implementation of different – often quite opposite – values, even if only within the area of strictly instrumental uses of knowledge. The same applies to descriptive findings. Nevertheless one should clearly distinguish the hypothetical uses of the results of sociological studies in various thinkable social conditions from their probable uses which can be more or less easily foreseen in a particular society at the given moment of its history. It seems it is these highly probable uses that should be taken primarily into consideration, because they delimit the use of the immediate social consequences of our studies. For instance, we are now witnessing an amazing development of certain branches of neurophysiology; but it is hard for many people to envision uses of findings or theories on the neurophysiology of the brain other than those which could serve for the 'physical control of mind'.[12] It is difficult in most contemporary societies to contemplate the uses of subliminal propaganda without fearing that it might be abused. Indeed, such possible uses of sociology are frightening some sociologists to the degree that they are ready to abandon the goal of developing theoretical social knowledge altogether, and to limit the tasks of sociology to strictly ideological functions. Let me quote again from the paper by P. Bandyopadhyay a fragment which in my opinion constitutes an answer to these fears:

> Conservatives since the Russian Revolution have burned countless

> gallons of midnight oil trying to refute the claims of social sciences correctly to analyze the societies of today and to provide rational foundations for socialist development. Indeed they have often denied the claims of social science itself. They have usually argued this in terms of the impossibility of objectivity, the necessary intrusion of values, the falsity of determinist analysis and therefore of predictions. They have inveighed against 'scientism' and the necessity for revolutionary times. It has been the radicals among the makers of social science who have championed and labored to prove the connection between the objective social sciences and the necessity for social science and socialism. Today, in North America at least, the positions seem reversed. Some conservatives proclaim the possibility of objective predictive social sciences, and radicals deny this possibility. In doing so, however, the radicals are in strange company: that of the conservatives of yesterday, still toiling to complete objective social science, bury Marx yet again and invalidate the laws of social development.
>
> This would be a matter for laughter were it not that the stakes are so high: the scope of reason, the comprehensibility of history and society, and the transformation of society in the direction of the fullest possible realization of equal freedom of all. It is, therefore, a great disservice to radicalism to adopt positions that conservatives have adopted in defense of the status quo on the basis of none-too-convincing arguments.[13]

To this admonition one can only add that positions which reject the possibility of the use of social theories for good purposes are extremely pessimistic, whereas radical values have traditionally been the elements of an optimistic attitude toward the world.

Some writers propose a special solution to this dilemma by the undertaking of so-called 'action research' which develops certain theories of very low generality, the intended applicability of which is limited to a specific set of social goals.[14] I think this combination of research and action toward the improvement of social reality is an extremely interesting phenomenon in contemporary sociology. It is interesting for many reasons. First of all, it acknowledges the need for direct involvement in socially meaningful actions on the part of sociology. And it also indicates that some important problem areas of social theory have not been sufficiently studied by sociology, so that the hypotheses needed for the guidance of action have to be tested in the course of the action itself. While the first aspect of action research is very encouraging, the second should be viewed as an unavoidable necessity only. The situation here is similar to that of a doctor who has to cure a patient when neither the diagnosis nor the remedies are to be found in the medical textbooks but must be found in the course of the medical action research. Such action research may be very stimulating for the development of medical knowledge, but any patient who makes an interesting case from this point of view knows very well that he has no particular reason to be happy about it. It is much safer for the patient to belong to a category of cases which are described by current medical theory. It is – in exactly the same way – much safer for a social group or society to have the kinds of social problems that have been analyzed before, and the nature and theoretical mechanisms of which are relatively well known, than for its problem to have to be solved by a theory the validity of which is being tested in the course of the action itself.

This does not mean I am against involvement of sociologists in socially meaningful practical actions aimed toward the improvement or change of social reality. Nor am I against action research when the existing theory is not sufficient for guiding practical social actions. I do not accept however, an attitude which regards action research as a substitute for so-called traditional research aimed toward the verification of social theories. Action research is not a substitute for but a supplement to regular research, and both these kinds of research can and should contribute to the development of sociological theories. And the better our theory the more efficient are its applications, and the more beneficial it will be for the societies, provided its applications are guided by proper social values.

Moreover, if the theoretical conclusions of any piece of action research are really empirically valid, we do not have any guarantee that they will not be used in the service of other – even quite opposite – social values, as is possible (at least theoretically) with any true finding or generalization.

While I disagree with those who propose to take sociology out of theorizing altogether, or to limit it to action research situations, I would like at the same time to oppose strongly any form of social or moral unconcern. I think in the first place that any sociologist who undertakes an applied social research task ordered by a 'client' (whether this be a social group, an institution or a person), and which is aimed toward the realization of certain gaols, by implication accepts these goals and assumes moral co-responsibility for their eventual realization. Secondly, I think it is a sociologist's obligation to try to foresee the possible consequences or uses of his work according to his best assessment of the social forces operating in the given society – the value systems, etc. – and to formulate his research problem with the clearest possible picture of both its cognitive and its social significance vis-a-vis his own value system. *If it should happen in some instance that he is able to foresee only an application of his theory that he cannot approve morally, I think he should abandon this particular avenue of inquiry. While it is our task to develop social knowledge, it is an even more important task not to develop it in situations where its misuse can be easily foreseen and would have dangerous social consequences.* The medical principle 'primum non nocere' – 'above all, not to do harm' – should be printed on the first pages of all our textbooks.

The postulate of social awareness is necessary but not sufficient in the case of sociology. We should encourage and develop within sociology a branch of sociological reflections and studies which could help us to understand better the possible instrumental utility of sociological findings and theories in different social contexts and for different value orientations – and thus to foresee better who is likely to use 'our sociology' and for what purposes. The development of just such a branch of sociology as this is for me of the greatest social importance.

VI. THE IDEOLOGICAL FUNCTIONS OF SOCIOLOGY

By an ideology we usually mean a set of fairly general values, some more specific evaluations of certain areas of reality when the knowledge about them is confronted with the more general evaluative standards, often some philosophical assumptions and beliefs, some more or less general descriptive and theoretical propositions referring to this reality and – last but not least – certain prescribed patterns of action aimed toward the conservation or change of reality. Some of the components of ideology have the character of empirically testable propositions, whereas others are of a normative character. But when we speak of the ideological functions of scientific – i.e. empirically testable – sociological propositions we usually mean the impact of these propositions or of some other empirical proposition which do not belong to ideology upon evaluative and motivational areas or ideologies, and especially the degree and direction in which they may influence human evaluations and motivations to specific actions, as well as the degree to which they may be able to integrate these actions in a collective effort toward a commonly accepted goal. Let us look first at the motivational functions of social sciences, at their role in triggering individual and collective actions.

To begin with, we can say that when diagnostic knowledge is able to trigger some motivational mechanisms aiming toward social actions, theoretical knowledge can orient such actions, channeling them toward the realization of means necessary for the implementation of the goals. Sometimes discovery of a theory may itself play the role of a motivational trigger mechanism. When the existence of a problem has been known for a certain time but no means were known which might be used for its solution, theoretical discoveries which reveal the *possibility* of a solution can start the motivational mechanisms and integrate individual motivations into one collective action.

In some situations the theoretical knowledge can even have a strong impact upon values. There might be many things we would like to have, frustrations we would like to eliminate, goals we would not object to realizing – but since we do not believe these things are possible, they exist as dreams somewhere on the periphery of our value system, scarcely belonging to it, and certainly not motivating our behavior. If it were to be discovered by a theoretician that they could be realized, that the means leading to them are such and such, and if additionally it should turn out that these means are within our range, it is very likely that this would lead to a basic change in the structure of our value system. The dreams would become real social goals with a powerful motivational force. On the other hand, if it could be proven that something we were aiming at is beyond the range of practical possibilities, this would probably lead to a decrease in the attractiveness of such a goal. In most instances, however, our theoretical analysis will be of a somewhat different kind. Our theories will say that realization is more or less probable and that the means necessary for it are more or less 'expensive' in the broad sense of the term. Such statements, of course, may also have some impact upon the attractiveness of the goal and may to different degrees influence human motivations.

One should remember that we are speaking here about certain socio-psychological mechanisms determining the impact of knowledge upon human evaluations and motivations. Some of these mechanisms correspond more or less closely to the pattern that is described in psychology as rational reasoning and rational behavior, but this does not mean that other psychological mechanisms cannot operate here. Thus for instance we observe in the formation of evaluations certain simple mechanisms described by theories of learning: e.g. when we discover in our theoretical analysis that a certain state of affairs is instrumental for some our goals, we see that a positive value is being attributed to this means too. It is even likely that due to the functional autonomization of instrumental values, the phenomena which were primarily seen as the means only will become positive values in themselves quite independently of the goals to which they were supposed to lead. Their instrumentality is often forgotten and ultimately they are treated as independent goals.

In other cases we see the operation of mechanisms that are fairly distant from the ideal of human rationality. According to elementary logic the same object when regarded from the standpoint of its various properties, and confronted with an identical set of evaluative standards, may be good from the standpoint of some of its properties and bad from the standpoint of others. We may arrive of course at some general evaluation of this object, taking into account its diverse partial evaluations without violation of the rules of rationality. But we also know that on a mass scale people feel uneasy when confronted with such instance of cognitive dissonance and tend to accept only some of the evaluations – those which go in only one emotional direction – and not to accept the others. This usually leads to the rejection of all dissonant information. Finally, from a strictly rational viewpoint, the concrete evaluations should be functions of our knowledge and our general normative standards, and the rules for actions should be derived from these premises jointly. We know, however, that many people behave otherwise. They will adapt the general evaluative standard to the requirement of a concrete evaluation if this concrete evaluation is somehow important to them, or they will be unwilling to admit any information that would make the acceptance of both the general evaluative standard and the concrete evaluation impossible. They may also be inclined to look for proper information necessary as rationalizations of action, rather than true information for use as a guide in their behavior.

Here I would like to mention one type of conclusion that is often encountered in discussions about the ideological implications of certain theories. If theory is understood as a set of general propositions describing the relations between the variables, such theory may be used instrumentally for the implementation of certain social goals – as discussed above – but it cannot justify, at least within the rules of rational thinking, any such goals without additional value judgment. By the same token, it cannot be used without such normative assumptions for either the justification of the status quo or the recommendation of social change. If the theory is believed to have such implications this is because these value assumptions are – usually unconsciously – taken for granted.

This can be especially clearly seen in recent discussions about the 'conservative assumptions' of functionalism, where the critics of functionalism failed to perceive that it has such conservative implications – for conservatives only. In criticizing the critics I do not have in mind, of course, specific evaluations of certain institutions made by representatives of the functionalist school or their general view of 'social equilibrium' as a desirable social goal. What I do defend is the general problem area of functionalism, which stresses the importance of looking for the social functions of different cultural patterns and institutions, and leaves (or should leave) open the problem of acceptance of these functions and of various kinds of social equilibrium. The conclusions to be drawn as to the appropriate social actions must be based on the confrontation of these empirically assessed functions with different human values.

The psychological mechanisms which determine the formation of evaluations may, when acting on a mass scale, influence the reception of sociological knowledge in such a way that the ideological conclusions formed from the sociologist's work are more or less distant from the ideal of human rationality. These mechanisms may also be used by various groups or institutions which, more or less deliberately, will try to derive from the sociologist's work conclusions which it does not justify, in order to influence attitudes and motivations on a mass scale. Finally – and which is most dangerous here – the need to influence attitudes by means of certain sociological information may lead to greater or lesser pressure upon sociologists to deliver independently of its truth information necessary from the standpoint of its specific ideological function, and to suppress certain other information even if it is true. I noted earlier that for strictly instrumental purposes, false information is useless. But – unfortunately – this is not the case with the ideological functions of sociology, because any information which is believed to be true by its 'receiver' will have an impact upon their attitudes and actions, either within the scheme of strictly rational thinking or according to any other kind of psychological mechanism. Therefore, if a group or institution is more interested (consciously or unconsciously) in influencing these attitudes in an a priori direction than in shaping them in an empirically justified, rational way, and at the same time possesses means of moral, economic or more direct pressure upon the sociologist, it may try to use these means to influence his enquiry in the desired direction.

Of course it may happen that such a group will profit from such misuse of sociology in the short term. But in the long run such behavior is usually irrational even from the standpoint of the values which underlay the pressure, because short-term gain in shaping human attitudes cannot compare to the costs of acting under a false diagnosis of the situation, and guided by the wrong theoretical assumptions. In practice this means that actions undertaken under such circumstances are either unnecessary or inefficient or both. It may also mean not undertaking action when action is necessary. It is also my firm belief that a sociologist who, sharing the values of some group yields to its pressure with respect to the form or content or presentation of his results does not do a service but an injury to the cause he believes in.

When these pressures are perceived by the scientist as coming from outside he is in a relatively better position to resist them. But when they act on him in a situation where he is a member of the pressuring group, and thus presumably accepts its values, he may yield more or less unconsciously. In such case the danger of diminishing the cognitive and instrumental value of his study – even from the standpoint of precisely the values he accepts – is especially serious. It seems that *the more we are engaged in a value system, and the more we are involved in the realization of the social goals determined by these values, and the more important the goal of our social action is to us, the more we should be alert to possible disturbances of the objective validity of our perceptions, analyses, and interpretations.* Above all, we should remind ourselves that nothing is more harmful for the realization of social goals than wishful thinking. Therefore, any increase of our value-involvement in the realization of certain social goals should be accompanied by an increase in our willingness to realize these goals by means of all the possibilities offered by objective scientific investigation.

Remembering that whatever we do may have an impact upon the thinking of those who are not specialists in our field and that only some of their conclusions may be rational, we should also try to stress the rules of correct inference in the presentation of our findings. One of the important tasks of the sociologist is to eliminate as much as he possibly can misinterpretations of his work, taking into account all the known mechanisms of the sociology and psychology of knowledge and trying to counteract them if they would lead in the wrong direction. Another equally important task is to make 'premeditated ideological misuses' of his study as difficult as possible.

All of this does not mean the sociologist is not entitled to evaluate the societies he is studying. Any human being has a 'right' to his values, and the sociologist is in no way obliged to be 'unhuman' here. For any human being – including the sociologist – it is quite legitimate to undertake actions aimed toward the realization of his values. And he is also entitled to communicate his values to all who are inclined to listen, as well as to those whose interest has not been aroused. But as a scientist he has some obligations which I would not hesitate to call moral ones. He must present as empirically valid only such facts and theories as have been discovered or tested in empirical investigations, adjusting the strength of his assertions to the strength of the empirical evidence supporting them. Whenever he enters the area of 'loose' theorizing or hypothetical speculations – both of which are necessary and important in the development of any science – he should not pretend that these constitute tested theories. Whenever he evaluates an area of social reality he should present his values distinctly from the assessed facts, leaving it to the reader or listener to accept the general values and concrete evaluations apart from the facts, or possibly to come to different evaluations on the basis of the same facts. Finally, when proposing some course of social action he should specify both the value assumptions which underlie his proposing or accepting certain goals and the theoretical and diagnostic findings which legitimize the proposed course of action. *Such a sociology would be at the same time both objective and value involved.* Its strictly cognitive components would develop in a cumulative process, in which we would obtain better and better understanding of this part of empirical reality that we call 'society'. This in itself might constitute a legitimate goal of study for those scientists guided by predominant cognitive motivations, provided they do not overlook the possible 'misuses' of their science. Such an objective yet value-involved sociology could also serve as an intellectual tool toward the transformation of our world into one such as we would like to live in. We will need for all of this a great deal of the theoretical and diagnostic knowledge which sociology can eventually give us, assuming its optimal scientific development. And we need as well some additional knowledge about the relations of sociology to society, its possible instrumental and ideological functions, in order to guide the development of our discipline in a wise way – so that it can be properly used and hardly ever abused. The faster we develop our discipline with respect to these criteria, the better for our social causes and for mankind in general.

NOTES

[1] Amando de Miguel: Sociology in an Authoritarian Society: A Pessimistic Reflection on the Case of Spain. Chapter 2 in this volume.

[2] See e.g. A. W. Gouldner, *The Coming Crisis of Western Sociology* (New York, Basic Books, 1970).

[3] P. Bandyopadhyay, 'One Sociology or Many', *Science and Society,* **XXXV**, No. 11, Spring, 1971, 1-2.

[4] See e.g. the paper by P. Bandyopadhyay cited above. See also H. S. Becker and I. L. Horowitz, 'Radical Politics and Social Research; Observations on Methodology and Ideology', *American Journal of Sociology,* 78, No. 1, July, 1972.

[5] F. Ferrarotti, 'Introductory Comments on the Theme: Is There a Crisis in Sociology?', Chapter 1 in this volume.

[6] For the analysis of some problems related to the formulation of reductive theories in sociology see S. Nowak, 'The Logic of Reductive Systematizations of Social and Behavioral Theories', in S. Nowak, *Understanding and Prediction: Essays in the Methodology of Social and Behavioral Theories,* to be published by D. Reidel Publishing Company.

[7] See 'Concepts and Indicators in Humanistic Sociology', in *Understanding and Prediction: Essays in the Methodology of Social and Behavioral Theories.*

[8] For a detailed discussion of logical and empirical relations

between the indicators and the indicated phenomena denoted by the given theoretical concept, see 'Concepts and Indicators in Humanistic Sociology', op. cit.

[9] For a closer analysis of the empirical assumption, involved in the formulation of questions of different kinds, see J. Gedymin, *Problemy zaozenia, rozstrzygniecia* [Problems assumptions solutions], Poznan, 1964. See also S. Nowak, *Methodology of Sociological Research,* Ch. I. The Formulation of the Research Problem and the Choice of the Right Methods. In Press. D. Reidel, Dordrecht, Holland.

[10] By a direct answer I mean an answer which does not abolish the validity of the assumptions of the given question. In the case of the above example, an indirect answer might be: 'Neither the system of social control, nor the community of values of its members contributes to the integration of this society. In fact this society is not integrated at all.' Such an answer would abolish the validity of the assumptions of our question. In some cases, when we conduct our study stepwise, the facts established at its first stage are used as the assumptions for the next question. The most simple example would be a series of interview questions: 'Do you have children?' 'If yes, how many?' The weakest form of assumption is that the phenomena in question at least might exist. Therefore we ask people about their children, but we do not ask them how many horns they have. (See: J. Gedymin, op. cit.).

[11] Unless we define our concept as referring to an 'ideal type', which does not exist in reality, but the postulation of which is useful heuristically in the formulation of our theory. In such a case we assume that the empirical phenomena may be ordered as different approximations to our ideal type and that such ordering is fruitful from the theoretical point of view.

[12] See E. Delgado, *Physical Control of Mind* . . . . .

[13] P. Bandyopadhyay, op. cit., 21-22.

[14] Quoted from mimeographed text of his introductory paper to the Symposium at the VIIIth World Congress of Sociology. See chapter 1 in this volume.

[15] See e.g. A. W. Gouldner, op. cit.

7

AN END TO SOCIOLOGY? with a SELECTED BIBLIOGRAPHY

Norman Birnbaum
Amherst College
and *Institute for Advanced Study, Princeton, New Jersey, USA*

No international sociological congress I have attended (and I have been at every one since 1953) has neglected the question, Is there a crisis in sociology? Upon occasion, the question has pervaded, even dominated, formal congress discussion. Upon others, it has constituted a substratum of criticism, in contrast with the certainties expressed in the official

---

Author's Note: My talk during the Toronto round table was delivered from notes, which of course I have used in writing this paper. I have attempted, however, to preserve the discursive style of the original; that has not been altogether difficult. I reserve for a later date a return to these problems – which is to say, I propose, shortly, to write a book about them, to continue work done under a Fellowship from the John Simon Guggenheim Memorial Foundation, which I gratefully acknowledge. In the meantime, those who consider this essay too theoretical, who think of sociology's task as primarily descriptive, might console themselves at the movies. Film-makers do more to bring contemporary society to an awareness of itself than anyone else. I once had doubts about that proposition, but after my valued colleague (and ex-student) Geoffrey Hawthorn compared a book of mine unfavorably to Haskell Wexler's *Medium Cool,* I reflected on it. Hawthorn did have a point. A selective Bibliography is attached.

proceedings. We may doubt our methods of social observation, despair of our interpretative ideas, deplore the use (or non-use) society makes of our work. No matter, we may console ourselves with obsessive self-concern. The participants in panels of this kind may change (although some, like their answers, may grow more familiar). The societies and types of regime they represent may vary. Their rhetoric, the saliency of some rather than other issues, may alter. We have now institutionalized the crisis. Systematic introspection, nay inversion, is a legitimate (and certainly, recognizable) disciplinary specialty. In this, we are not entirely alone. Economists, historians of literature, historians *tout court*, philosophers can be heard discussing their own work in what appear to be similar terms. Aestheticians ask if art has ended, and some if psychiatry has become anti-psychiatry. The difficulties within our field partake of a general crisis in the human sciences. Profound historical change and its (distorted) reflection in thought seem inextricable.

It apparently remains only for all of us in the human sciences to look enviously at the natural scientists, whose problems of conceptual discontinuity seem to offer happier resolutions. Perhaps our envy is closely related to our unfamiliarity with these sciences, themselves undergoing deep and rapid transformation. Perhaps, as we shall see, the analysis of these transformations may tell us something about ourselves. But *Schadenfreude* over the fate of colleagues whose concerns are near to ours, envy of those whose discourse seems entirely different, are equally easy, even cheap. What is hard, and necessary, is another examination of our own difficulties. And chief amongst these is our propensity to suppose that our crisis has a solution. We would do well to begin by thinking of it historically, and asking if it has a beginning and a middle: the end may be different from any we can envisage ahistorically. To anticipate a bit, many of us had hitherto supposed that the trouble was that sociology had the wrong ideas. Consider, however, the possibility that the idea of a sociology as a separate discipline is in itself wrong?

I. ORIGINS AND PROGRESSION

Sociology developed in the nineteenth century as a response to the deficiencies of the traditional modes of apprehending society. Political philosophy often (think of Rousseau and Burke, De Maistre and Mill) entailed models of society, images of comportment, analyses of motivation. Its strength was, however, its weakness. The abstract qualities of the tradition of political philosophy allowed the historical concreteness of modern social development to escape. Of course, it pervaded political philosophy – by reflection and refraction. However, themes like the antithesis between tradition and emancipation were addressed with contemporary reference subordinated to the analysis of principles.

The abstract quality of political economy was, by contrast, an advantage. It is customary for moralists (and others) to denounce political economy for obsessive concern with homus economicus. In a society in which new forms of production and exchange converted much of society into an appendage of the market, this concern was precondition for intellectual achievement – as Marx saw. Sociology, in the work of Comte and Spencer, and later of Toennies and Durkheim, inquired into the consequences of that transformation. In doing that, however, the new mode of inquiry often detached itself (by a curious intellectual progression) from a concern with the market.

The claim of history to be the totalizing discipline par excellence (even in epochs in which a political historiography was dominant) cannot be discounted.. However, history's mode of totalizing a description of society was concrete – a single historical situation examined, brought into focus. Moreover, historians were interested in the past as a precondition of the present; they very rarely described the present as a result of the past. Marx, it will be recalled, disclaimed credit for the discovery of the importance of social classes in modern history – attributing that to the liberal Guizot. Sociology, with its sense of the uniqueness of the emergent industrial and capitalist society, might have understood itself as a form of contemporary history. (De Tocqueville's self-understanding was approximately that.) Instead, the analysis of that society schematized history. In the effort to fix the outlines of a new epoch, the presence of the legacy of the past was overlooked.

Finally, there was Politikal Arithmetik, Kameralistik, la Physique Sociale – the efforts to quantify observable social regularities. Much of the historical energy concentrated in these new forms of thought was to end in political economy. The response to quantification of the first generations of sociologists was not unequivocal. Some treated these developments as techniques, useful ancillaries to social interpretation. None, not even Comte, supposed that the total quantification of sociological analysis was now possible. Even those most influenced by the natural sciences (Comte and Mill) concentrated on the development of very general categories which could subsume qualitative data. I refer to matters like the construction of theories of consensus and cohesion, attributions of motivational sequence. Spencer, of course, used evolutionary (biological) models. Let us take seriously the familiar argument that it was Malthus' model of population that influenced Darwin, conceptions of nature imitating ideas of society and not the other way around. It was as an idea, not as a rigorous model of discourse, that the notion of natural limits entered sociology. If Weber, for instance, was a social Darwinist, metaphor and not technique infused his work.

Sociology, then, was from its inception an exceedingly synthetic discipline. It brought political philosophy up to date by attempting to objectify some of the moral dilemmas which pre-occupied that sort of inquiry. That is, it historicized conflicts which were once depicted as immutable. From political economy, sociology drew the idea of the novelty, the magnitude, of the market. History gave it a sense of movement, of sequence. Social statistics, finally, supplied the elements of a concrete description of the armature of the new society. We may put the matter in another way. Sociology attempted a description of a new social formation *sui generis.* That description, however, was fused to analysis – which derived statements about the new social formation from general principles of social behavior and social process. These principles, however, were often enough expressions of conceptions historically specific to the new nineteenth century society. The synthesis, briefly, rested upon the delicacy and justice of the historical perceptions of the first sociologists. We should not be surprised that no sooner promulgated, the synthesis began to break down.

The breakdown was, conceptually, very nearly complete by the time sociology was admitted to the academy. I am unconvinced that the resistance to the introduction of sociology in the universities (very recently overcome in the case of the ancient British universities, about which I know a bit) was due to trivial academic interests. It had two sources, and only a thinker committed to simplistic reductionism would attribute primacy to one or the other. The first was the movement of thought. The methodological, or philosophical, assumptions, the substantive concepts, the techniques of observation and analysis, of the human sciences may and did exhibit a near-chaotic diversity. They also constituted a field of considerable intellectual riches, few of which sociology seemed capable of appropriating. Think, for instance, of the fact that our field has never really assimilated psychoanalysis or (more recently) structural linguistics.

The second was the movement of society. The lineaments of industrial society having been seized, they changed. New densitites, new mechanisms, new institutions, emerged. No one account (or model) seemed able to encompass these. Further, in contemporary politics, ideas of and about society were political artefacts. Conflict within sociology expressed, often in distorted or foreshortened form, conflicts of a political kind. The scientific pretensions of many sociologists, and even more their scientific perspectives, compelled them to flee the implications of this condition. At its inception, sociology sought to complete the task of political philosophy. During its (spurious) maturity, it abandoned that task. As a result, where sociology was not morally and intellectually impoverished, it was historically disoriented. Viewing things *sub speciae aeternaitatis,* sociologists lost their capacity to see them in their historical specificity.

In the middle period of sociology, after the generation of Durkheim, Pareto and Weber, there were three central tendencies. The first, certainly quantitatively the most important, was a concentration on specific sectors of modern society. Stratification (not class), urban and rural sociologies, analyses of the family, industrial studies, became the central matter of sociological investigation. Whereas previous generations had used data of this sort as material for the construction of ideas of society in its totality, a new asceticism now made its appearance.

Comte was attached to scientific method (or scientistic, in the view of intelligent detractors like von Hayek) but insisted that he had a view of the social totality. His twentieth century descendants claimed that they would generate a view of the whole, after an indefinite series of specific inquiries. There was no agreed conception of the scope of these inquiries. Some envisaged the testing of general hypotheses on social behavior and process. Others thought of concentration on specific sectors of society, depicted as more (or less) central to the functioning of the whole. All agreed that a sociological utopia lay in the future. At some point, the discipline would promulgate valid knowledge of society as a whole.

The utopia to be constructed in this way certainly represented an identification of sociology with the process of rationalization. Every bit of metaphysical pathos was banished from the field. The ancient chores of political philosophy were assigned to other specialists, themselves often all too eager to abandon them.

The third tendency was another, a secular substitute, for political philosophy. A series of general, if contradictory, characterizations of the epoch was produced by sociologists self-consciously engaged in historical commentary. The names of Mannheim and Sorokin will suggest the varied scope of the enterprise. We can look back and see that Weber, himself an historical commentator of great power, provided precept and example for the enterprise. The separation of judgement of fact from judgement of value, the dizzying discrepancy between his conceptual analysis of human action and his historical work, suggest that Weber accepted as ineluctable the fragmentation of sociological vision.

Contemporary sociology is the legatee of this progression. Certainly, most of its effort continues in the area of sectorial studies of modern society. Appearance and reality are different. It appears that sociologists study matters ignored by others (other disciplines, the general public). In fact, sociology has a peculiar sensitivity to changes in the mood of the technocratic directorates who dominate (as best they can) our epoch. In the United States, to take three recent instances, the exacerbation of the problem of blacks and other minorities, the complex of questions around impoverishment, the protest of students and youth, were not anticipated by sociologists. Attention was given to these matters when they attracted political attention. Much of modern sociology (and this is as true in the state socialist societies, if not more so) makes of it a data-gathering component of highly fallible social technology. The scientific utopia of which I spoke fools almost no one. The interest in contemporary sociology is not due to its putative capacity for large-scale social description, but to its actual ability to eschew that in order to collect administratively useful knowledge.

The making of social theory continues, nevertheless. It increasingly resembles that preoccupation with an historically contentless totality, a model of all possible societies, anticipated by Durkheim. Interestingly, recent work on Durkheim shows how this was a pendant to his own belief in a social technology. What is so striking about social theory today is its abstracted capacity. A *machine à tout faire,* it serves everyone and no one. The epoch of functionlist domination of social theory is over, at least for the United States (perhaps it is just beginning in the Soviet Union, where an enforced consensus is a political fact). We have, instead, a *mélange* of methodological argument, alternative categorical systems, competing images of society. But, wait: have I not just insisted on the abstracted quality of contemporary theoretical discussion, with the implication that it continued at least one of sociology's recent traditions, the flight from political philosophy? Do not competing images of society, if my term has any meaning, imply the return of political discussion? Indeed they do. I will not write of a return of the repressed, since it is unclear that this particular return is actually a therapeutic recovery. It may be what the psychoanalysts term, acting out.

The element of historical commentary in contemporary sociology is the *via regis* for the incorporation of a kind of political philosophy in our work. Statements on the possibilities and limits of development of our society, upon analysis, are frequently statements of political choice. (Consider the controversy on the specificity of a post-industrial society, Bell and Touraine inter alia identifying it in entirely different ways.) Politics, of a sort, even saturates the data gathering operations of those who think of themselves as technologists of research; as pure empiricists. Ideas of our historical location (and therewith, ideas of the kind of polity we can attain) set the limits, and often fix the content, of the categories in which data are recorded. Indeed, the categories form the data. The long debate in another part of sociology which opposed conflict theorists to consensual ones ought not to be dismissed as a poor successor to medieval scholasticism. Historians of scholasticism, after all, tell us that even technical argument on points of minor detail evoked structural differences within and between medieval philosophical systems. We can understand that debate as a form of political controversy. That some of the participants in it did not dare utter its name is regrettable, but not of overwhelming account.

II. THE INELUCTABLE CRISIS

The distinguished members of the panel have indeed agreed that there is a crisis in sociology. They are agreed neither on its dimensions, precise historical causes, or philosophical and political meanings. For every sociologist, a crisis: the discipline which claimed at the beginning to adumbrate a new social-historical totality ends in a plurality, if not an infinity, of opinions. A metaphysical bang ends with a methodological whimper. Surely, more can be said; it follows.

The differences expressed here are important, not because they are easy of resolution, but because they may not be. One element of the crisis in sociology seems clear – we ask too much of it. How can a single discipline integrate all of contemporary knowledge in the human sciences, give an exact account of the inner movement of contemporary world history, provide the idea of a good or fulfilled human community, derive the socio-political techniques which would bring that community into being, and resolve every contradiction and difficulty in the contemporary theory of knowledge?

A simple solution presents itself: ask less. That would be simple, but inelegant. Each problem on the list has this characteristic – it entails every other. Limiting the central problem of sociology to one is not a way to avoid any of the others. What we do need at first is a process of clarification, in which we could become aware of the systematic interrelations amongst these problems. Therapeutic clarification for individuals takes the form of educating them to assume inner responsibility for their acts, as a preliminary to any change in their behavioral pattern. A conceptual therapy for sociologists would invite them to recognize that they cannot escape responsibility for the intellectual consequences of their interests. I propose to proceed by sketching the universe of discourse sociology entails. I will then ask what assistance, if any, we may ask of other sorts of inquiry: there is much that we have to learn. Finally, I will consider the idea of crisis again: by then, an answer may be less difficult.

Left and right, the party of change and the party of order, have marched their armies across our stage for so long that we have lost sight of something: their struggle is often illusory. Lecture room Metternichs and literary Robespierres have this in common, a penchant for pursuing theoretic discussion of politics ad absurdam. Reading some sociological polemics, one might think that society as a whole had entrusted custody of political ideology exclusively to committees of sociologists (or, at least, academics). It would follow that everything sociologists did has political implications. That is, perhaps, true – but not in the way it is commonly understood. Political clarification in sociology takes the form of self-clarification, looking for the political implications of sociological analysis. Would it not be more efficacious to add to this a different sort of effort, to understand the political implications of ostensibly apolitical aspects of social process? This might well imply two sorts of analysis. The one would deal with the interpenetration of politics and ordinary institutions. The phrase is cumbersome: politics is not a separate institutional sphere in modern societies, and there are in any event no ordinary institutions. I do not refer to the struggle for power within institutions, taken discretely, but to the ways in which these struggles combine into a pervasive politics. All of politics, additionally, is not struggle: the constraints which canalize conflict in one rather than another direction, mobilize or immobilize energies, are as important as overt antagonisms. A total system of social constraints, therefore, sets limits on the polity. What these limits are, and how they could be extended, are important questions for a sociology that would think of itself as political.

I have said that, until now, historical commentary has been the usual mode of integration of political philosophy with sociology. Would it not be more economical to attempt that integration, which now proceeds in haphazard and unreflective fashion, in a more direct way? Some prefer an advocacy social science, with social scientists taking the side of hitherto oppressed or disadvantaged groups. I do not consider it a denigration of the enterprise to suggest that it entails but one interpretation of politics, and of knowledge. A technocratic politics of the left, very little different in texture from that of the right, may be a result. In any case, an image of political community as a vacuum into which competing interests rush would accept, and perhaps reify contemporary political structures in the liberal capitalist societies. Suppose, alternatively, that sociology were to concern itself with different models of political community, new forms of representation, new sorts of public education and exchange of opinion, qualitative conceptions of the public interest. Neither all nor much of this need point in the direction of decentralization: our societies present problems in the identification, as well as the control, of centralized power. It is surprising how little that is not schematic sociologists have to say about these problems. Our idea of techno-bureaucratic society is unilinear, presupposing the alternation of uninterrupted growth of a central steering apparatus and spasmodic guerilla actions against it. A useful relationship between our conceptions of political possibility and our philosophical notions of political ends requires a dialectical confrontation.

Is this a way of asking that sociologists become political philosophers? I do not think so, but it is a way of asking that we take stock of the political philosophical component in our thought. That is a matter larger than our taking sides in present conflicts. It involves critical reflection on the range of analytic discourse to which our fascination with immediate structures of conflict restricts us. We will have to recognize that different conceptions of human substance, of sociability itself, may involve amended or new analytic categories. The kind of thought at issue need not exhaust itself in the construction of utopias. We would do well to recognize that the imagination required for utopian thought may be a working element in any sociological thinking that would go beyond our parochialisms. History does generate changes in consciousness: it is time that instead of running after history, we anticipated somewhat.

Historical anticipation obliges us to explore the developmental possibilities of our political structures. The analysis of possibility, in turn, sends us back to the subtle transformations of power in our society, in which form and content have come apart. Some part of the uneasiness of the advanced societies comes from the sense that they are out of control. There is a pervasive bad conscience amongst politicians and their intellectual servitors which bespeaks their awareness of the discrepancy between their world historical pretensions and their dwarf-like practise. A sociological analysis of power will have to relate dialectically to these tempers and distempers, as the bad conscience of their bad conscience. The search for new models of political community, however, cannot legitimate itself through its intentions. It will have to be judged on the plausibility and precision of its arguments.

Upon examination, philosophical openness calls for historical specificity. Larger systems of sociological interpretation have treated the successive transformations of bourgeois society in condensed fashion, distilling its experience into categories. We now know three things, if we know anything. Within these societies, the forms and substance of bourgeois domination are ending. We have reason to suspect that the conventional historical periodicization is wrong: different time scales, and other processes than those that dominated bourgeois self-depiction have shaped that progression whose outlines we thought we comprehended. Meanwhile, the global power exercised by the bourgeois nations has been drastically reduced. There is something quaintly archaic, indeed, about the term bourgeois to describe a historical formation we now suspect was at the intersection of a number of lines of development. I may put the problem in a different way, which connects with my discussion of political community. That the ideas of Aristotle, Augustine, Hobbes, Rousseau and Hegel have entered sociology, not by direct appropriation but by incorporation in a tradition of social theory of which we are the heirs is not surprising. What is surprising is that sociologists should suppose that our categories are universal, whereas others are historically specific. Just as our society is historically stratified, and can be read like an archaeological site, our thought bears the imprint of its origins.

It is customary to treat this problem under the rubric of ethnocentrism, rather as the political component of sociology may be depicted as a form of partisanship. These are simple terms of criticism and imply simple answers. The situation is much more complex. There can be no immediate leap from ethnocentrism to a pure universalism, just as there can be no total transition from political bias to value neutrality. Indeed, a pure universalism may not be value neutral, since it may well entail judgements on our part as to the direction in which social history should tend. We find ourselves in the midst of a historical and cultural process by which the elements of a new universalism are being developed, or – more precisely – argued and even fought about. A falsely totalizing discipline in its present form, sociology can at least accept the burden of constructing provisional totalizations of reflection. It is with some care that I have chosen the word *reflection*. Unless it is to claim to be that universal science uniting thought about society and thought about nature the emergence of which Marx predicted, sociology (or, rather, sociologists) must make more modest claims.

I have connected the analysis of our historicity and the depiction of political community, and I would justify the connection in this way. The decreasing degree of autonomy of function of separate societies, the situation of polycentric global conflict into which they have moved, gives us a world history as a series of increasingly interconnected particular histories. The spread of industrialization and ideas of citizenship might seem to suggest the westernization of the world (a phrase which is embarrassing in connection with the Chinese Revolution). It by no means suggests its modernization, a term which implies that our own societies are at the apex of human development. The specific historical forms of industrialization, the new political systems being developed in large parts of the world, can more fundamentally be read as evidence for the end of the western preponderance in world history. By analogy, the enormous increase in the functions of the modern state is by no means synonymous with an extension of its power. The interpenetration of state and society endows the state with a greatly enlarged task of coordination. It also enables a system of power integrated with the market to integrate itself in turn with the state.

The phrase, provisional totalization of reflection, needs explication. The provisional quality of sociological discourse would consist of a self-conscious process of historical localization. The categories of discourse would be understood as adapted to a specific unit of historical time. The totalizing aspect would rest on the effort to seize a phenomenon in its interconnectedness; distinctiveness could be established only in these terms. (It is not inappropriate, here, to recall the valuable work of the late Georges Gurvitch, ignored with sovereign provinciality in the English speaking world, so important in post-war France.) The term reflection would distinguish sociological thought from what the positivists term protocol statements, or from conceptions of knowledge derived from simplified ideas about laboratory science. The falsification of hypotheses is not the central task of the social sciences. Their task is the establishment of categories, of ideas of the sequence of social causation, in which hypotheses may be framed.

I have said that the problem is neither one of ethnocentrism nor of political partisanship, and by now it is perhaps somewhat clearer where the difficulty lies. The problem for sociological discourse is to transcend the intellectual objectifications of the various forms of ideological limitation-objectifications which have to be dealt with in their own terms as systems of discourse. Further, not all the limitations of vision and thought in sociology are ideological. Many stem from deficiencies in knowledge, rigour and imagination. Briefly, the corrective for deficient sociological discourse is more cogent discourse. In the third section of this paper, I will attempt to identify some of the contemporary sources of cogency in the social sciences, and their implications for sociology. For the moment, let us continue with this sketch of some of the components of discourse.

The question of ethnocentrism requires attention; it cannot be exorcised lightly. I may begin with the observation that the most resolutely anti-ethnocentric of contemporary social thinkers is, possibly, Lévi-Strauss. He does, after all, deny any privileged historical status to western rational thought and argues that in the sight of nature, all societies are alike (Lévi-Strauss is a secularized exponent of the thought uttered by Ranke, to the effect that all epochs were equal in the sight of God.) Yet it is Lévi-Strauss who claims that the categories imputed by himself to the savage mind are universal, that the structure of human thought in myth is precisely that, human. In other words, the assertion of ethnocentrism implies a conception of a common humanity expressing itself in some of its cultural and social structures. No communication between different groups, no understanding of other cultures, would be possible on any other bases. There is a similar problem with respect to anti-psychiatry. The attack by Laing and others on the assumptions of customary psychiatric diagnosis pre-supposes a more encompassing, a truer theory of human nature. The anti-psychiatrists on no account renounce the possibility of a theory, they insist that theirs is better.

Warnings about ethnocentrism do have a point, however. Our categories for the construction of ideas of society depend heavily upon western exprience. There is no language of all languages, and our notions of social development bear the imprint of our own. I have referred to the disastrous reliance of sociologists of development on concepts like modernization, which assumed (a) that every place would become like every other and (b) they would all resemble the United States. It is easier, now, to cast off this idea – not least because the United States bears little resemblance to our colleagues' ideas of it. When we consider events like the Cultural Revolution in China and the Cambodian Revolution, we can conclude that modern social development can and does take many courses. The very idea of development, indeed, is in question: Max Weber was right to have insisted that cultures could choose to rationalize ritual rather than industrial production. Machine production, in any event, does not predetermine a specific course of social development.

What of the theory of human nature itself? There is no work in sociology in this century (or any other) to compare in originality, profundity and explanatory power with that of Freud. The death of classical psychoanalysis, as therapeutic technique and as theory, has been announced often enough. In the absence of a plausible succession, it remains alive. A perfectly good argument can be made for the position that institutional analysis and inquiry into the bio-psychic sources of behavior are different. The difficulty is that analysts of institutions make assumptions about the sources of behavior: it was not so long ago that American functionalist sociology was full of adumbrations of the doctrine of tension reduction (a mechanical derivative of psychoanalytic theory which any conscientious student of Freudian texts would have to repudiate). One common alternative (found in the work of Parsons, despite his own great interest in psychoanalysis) was the idea that value systems and role prescriptions were capable of mobilizing and fixing a variety of psychological content. I have no doubt that the assertion is true, but it is one of those propositions which can tell us how a system works once it is established, appreciably less about the direction of change. Sociologists still need a theory of human nature, a specific grounding for the classical postulate that humans are political animals or species beings.

Comparative work on personality development was, in some measure, meant to show that the psychoanalytic model had a limited cultural and historical validity. The inquiry encountered two difficulties. The first was (and is) that some sort of psychological explanation had to be offered to replace psychoanalysis, and that none was forthcoming. The second was that the limitations did not seem to be so evident: the model held. Now psychohistory has come forward to replace the studies of culture and personality of twenty years ago. I defer an examination of its claims for some pages. For the moment, suffice it to remark that ad hoc theories of human nature (invented for the purposes of each inquiry or theory) confront us with a very large intellectual void.

The intellectual responsibilities of sociology involve us in epistemological discussions which are not the province of philosophers alone. Much of modern sociology proceeds as if the last word on method had been uttered by John Stuart Mill (another set of colleagues attests its devotion to tradition by acting as if the sixth volume of *The Positive Philosophy* were the summit of human thought). Mach has been referred to, and so has Reichenbach. Two simple propositions throw us, however, into disarray. The first is that the methods of the natural sciences do not apply without severe emendation to the social sciences. The second is that the natural sciences themselves are in the midst of an important reassessment of their methodological foundations. Some fields (neuroscience, primate evolution, ethology) look to the social sciences to complete their own lacunae. In the circumstances, a new map of learning has to be drawn – with impermanent frontiers, large extra-territorial enclaves, and uncharted oceans.

III. GREEN IN OTHER GARDENS

At times I have the impression that some of our colleagues

think that we are the only heirs of the hermetic tradition. Their vision, if it may be called that, of our field is of a self-contained theoretic system, with its own methods for gathering empirical data. It is quite true that sociology at its beginnings was concerned with what others left out. The first sociologists, however, thought that important matters had been omitted. The contemporary search for distinctiveness is likely to lead us into redundancy or triviality (or both). Many other fields of inquiry deal with social structure and social process, and where they do not, it is often the minimal importance of the phenomena that deters them.

If sociology once dealt with problems neglected elsewhere, it did not neglect the other sorts of inquiry. Many of the major figures in the brief history of sociological thought knew the economics, history and philosophy of their times. The recent self-containment of sociology may well be responsible for that lack of intellectual substance which is so troubling about our field. Perhaps the time has come to look for a solution to our difficulty or difficulties, if one can be found, beyond the usual academic borders. New ideas, new perspectives, the identification of new problems, may stimulate us to re-think our assumptions and directions. I am uncertain that new findings (insofar as these can be distinguished from new ideas) will do as much good. What the shocks of contemporary history and experience cannot do, scholarly papers are unlikely to accomplish. Alternative structures of thought may, however, influence our perceptions. Part II of this paper described some of the problems sociology has to face; this section suggests that there may be answers, if tentative ones, at hand.

The systematic study of politics, in an historical situation in which no institution, no aspect of culture, is shielded from social conflict, is a useful beginning point. Much recent literature on the interpretation of state and society suggests that our ideas of the distinction between sectors or institutions have to be revised. There was a period, before détente, when Americans and Western Europeans expended much conceptual energy on a phenomenon termed 'totalitarianism'. Some of us will persist in the belief that differences between societies, with respect to the freedom of political expression and organisation, are important matters. It is no less important to recognise that these freedoms may be attenuated, or require redefinition, in a society of pervasive political constraint. The preconditions of totalitarianism may be nearer home than we think.

The growth of public employment (and of unions of public service workers) makes of the modern state an arena of indirect social conflict. The services provided by the state are indispensable not only to the citizenry in general but to the controllers of large concentrations of productive property. In taking the benefits of public services, and paying little for them, they are engaged in a form of exploitation no less effective for being indirect. Conflict, however, opposes state to civil servant, civil servant to an amorphous public. Max Weber suggested, to the approval of later liberal epigones, that efforts by groups like the civil servants to make permanent their advantages could so alter market structures as to constitute a reintroduction of an estate society. Perhaps, but it would be no less appropriate to see in this development a displacement of struggles which in an earlier phase of capitalism occurred in the market.

Both processes, the politicisation of larger spheres of society and the simultaneous displacement and extension of market struggles, lend urgency to recent attempts to rethink the idea of a public interest. Nineteenth century sociology, with its insistence on the separation of state and society, may be thought of as an expression of a liberal idea of the public. In the epoch of the industrialisation of culture, ideologies and opinion are manufactured. It is difficult to sustain models of social structure which take consensus seriously. The sociology of culture has been thought of as a derivative of the serious task of analysing social structure. We may now ask if contemporary social structure demands more serious analyses of culture.

The tediousness of the counter-culture, its dreadfully hard work at play and its obvious inanities, ought not to obscure the importance of contemporary cultural protest. Dreitzel, in particular, has shown how the fragmentation of contemporary experience has combined with its rationalisation to generate counter movements. New forms of politics are, in his view, based on the body, on sexual differences, on unsatisfied religious impulses, on an irreducible hedonism which techno-bureaucratic society does not deny, but imperfectly canalises. Weber insisted on the primacy of the 'metaphysical needs of the human spirit'. It should not surprise cultural conservatives that these have made a sensational reappearance.

In another, but closely rclated, area, the crisis of the university impels us to rethink the relationship of knowledge to society. Knowledge is an essential component in administration and production. A series of events (some major like the Chinese Cultural Revolution, some relatively minor but significant like the disputes over research organisation and priorities in the US, France, and the United Kingdom) suggest that the relationship is political. Political analysis in the conventional categories does not often rise above description. The work of Habermas, his effort to redefine the Marxist theory of ideology by distinguishing between the categories of work and interaction, opens the way for a critical assessment of the social potential of knowledge. Habermas' effort in this sphere is connected of course with his inquiries into the structure and politics of communication.

Some critics have, unreasonably, accused Habermas of liquidating the Marxist tradition by reducing relationships of exploitation and domination to systems of communication. They are unreasonable, because Habermas has attempted the conceptual mastery of a development intrinsic to advanced societies: the internalisation of knowledge by the institutions of domination. That, in turn, has its counterpart in the internalisation of the fact of domination in our institutions of culture, and in their symbolic products. Certainly, the work of Gorz on the political determination of technical relationships in the division of labor (supported by the work of the American political economist Marglin) provides an empirical justification for Habermas' theoretical concerns. With due allowance for the differences induced by technical development, cultural structures, and political rhetoric, a serious Maoism would take the Starnberg branch of the Frankfurt School seriously. There can be no Cultural Revolution in the west without a new theory of knowledge in society. Habermas' work is political.

We can continue the discussion of new ideas about politics by turning to political economy. The force of inertia in human affairs is very great, and sociologists, like everyone else, underestimate it. The economists continue their work in universities, the private sector, and government – as their conceptual systems crash about our ears, as their refined methods exhibit a sustained incapacity to generate data with either a short-term or a long-term application. At least this generation of students in sociology will not have to listen to teachers who enjoin upon them the exemplary value of the work of our colleagues in economics. However the discomfiture of some economists need not be shared by all. Some did attempt analyses which would include the political contexts of the market, others insisted on the economy's status as an object of historical thought, still others dealt with the new world economy, the advanced forms of imperialism. Not all of the economists in this category are Marxists (it is entirely unclear that the hundreds of economists working on problems of capitalism in the state socialist regimes were less surprised by the current crisis than their western colleagues). One lesson of recent events is a negative one: no amount of technical sophistication or methodological refinement will compensate for erroneous ideas. Many economists, however, had and have ideas we must consider.

The first such group works on the extension of the market, that is, on the interpretation of state and economy. Its descriptions of resource allocation, of the struggle over state policy in areas like fiscal policy, tax structure, and the provision of public services provide us with a political sociology of modern society which does not limit itself to explicit political process and ideology. The obvious importance of these studies for questions of social policy make of them indispensable elements of a modern sociology of social classes. There is an honorable tradition in political economy, not all of it Marxist, of attention to the long-term problems of accumulation and economic structure. Simple examination will suggest how much of the work done by sociologists on stratification rests on changes in occupational and economic structure analysed by economists. I referred earlier to the industrialisation of cultural production. Sociologists for too long have criticised economists for their excessive attention to the market, and for their alleged lack of interest in social factors. Suppose, however, that much of society has become a market? Certainly, the political economists who have been studying imperialism have made possible a sociology of world society which could encompass the interpenetration of internal and external politics, phenomena like cultural domination and the role of the *compradores.*

We encounter *terra incognita.* Models of profit maximisation do not work when taken as a total description of any segment of world society. Notions of economic politics, of the maintenance of power, seem more appropriate – particularly when related to the behavior of those who control large concentrations of productive power. A theoretic synthesis exceeds our present capacities. Nothing, it is sure, can result from an artificial separation of sociologies of development from analyses of the world market. And a political sociology which assumes that the market is a separate entity cannot be taken seriously. Summum summarum, the actual structures of contemporary society do not lend themselves readily to theoretic apprehension. Their underlying unity, if any, has to be won from the data with models that possess some historical saliency.

If it can be said that the past decade has been one of theoretic and methodological confusion in sociology, some of our colleagues in history may have cause for self-satisfaction. The development in several countries of a sophisticated social history has stimulated work in the sociological tradition, and sometimes gone beyond it. There are two customary attitudes to the materials of history in sociology. One is that history supplies a large amount of data, which can be used to test timeless or universal propositions about social behavior. The other is that sociology's task is the ordering of historical sequence, sociological theory systematising history. When we seriously examine the claims of the historians of the 'Annales' group, a third possibility emerges: history elucidates the structures which sociologists study. History then, is a master discipline – because of its temporal scope and inclusiveness. A large claim, but no larger than recent claims made by sociologists – and one which, in the work of the Annales group, may well be true.

The insistence of the Annales historians on what Braudel terms 'la longue durée' does not ascribe any especial property to time. It rests on the observation that some important things in social existence, the development of contexts for specific events, the interaction of several causes to generate a structural effect, do take time. The Annales historians, then, study processes of historical accumulation. Their aim is the identification of underlying structures, the differentiation of short-term and long-term cycles, the location of points of discontinuity. Not surprisingly, in their view, what we think of as points of discontinuity often enough are culminations of perfectly regular series.

The Annales group has not confined itself to economic history, although its work in that area is striking: the depiction of accumulative cycles, the analysis of the interpenetration of economy, technology and demographic regulation. Perhaps its most distinctive contribution is the analysis of the combination of spheres: natural and human space, technology and productive organisation, economy and social structure, social structure and politics constituting related series. I use the term series rather than structure or system because the group succeeds so well in incorporating temporality in its organisation of the data of human activity. One of the concepts employed by the Annales group does have a unifying function – that of 'mentalités'. 'Mind' will not translate the term, nor will 'ethos', which is closer. 'Mentalité' is a cultural system, a set of values, a predisposition to response. In their 'mentalités' humans struggle with their environments, interpret their collective existence, appropriate the past and bring it, however unconsciously, to life. A Mentalité is a totalisation of historical constraint and historical possibility. In emphasising its importance, the Annales historians have not subscribed to an imprecise voluntarism. They have, instead, taken seriously the contemporary interest in the objective constraint exercised by symbolic structures, as analysed in the fields of aesthetics, comparative religions, psychoanalysis and structural linguistics. In joining the analysis of these structures to precise accounts of other historical series, the group practises a large social science.

This is an essay and not a treatise; neither is it a *bibliographie raisonée.* I have concentrated on the historians of the Annales group; they have a theoretical coherence which makes reference to their work simple. Of course, I could cite other historians, some of them well known to sociologists. Hobsbawm, Rudé and Thompson have revivified the interpretation of the growth of capitalism. Genovese and his colleagues in the United States, in their exploration of slavery, have obliged us to reconsider the nature of American society. There is a new body of work in Germany on the social origins of Nazism, and in Italy on fascism. Schorske's work on Vienna enables us to speak with more precision of the rationalisation of modern western culture, and Bailyn when dealing with eighteenth century politics in America tells us much of the migration of societies. The point is not to assimilate these works to a fixed corpus of doctrine in sociology, but to see how they change the terms of our discourse.

That is a result we usually expect of comparative studies in culture and society. As I ponder the vast literature on recent politics in the Third World, only a bare minimum of which I have read, I wonder to what extent some of it has the effect of a familiar self-fulfilling prophecy. The interpretation of development beyond the confines of western Europe and

North America with models of social analysis abstracted from our own development is perfectly comprehensible. It may, however, lead us to construct the data in sequences which miss some essential points.

A recent investigation of childhood in Soviet Russia suggested that the spheres of childhood and adulthood were closely connected in that society, and that children very early developed an explicit sense of the primacy of the group. An examination of the history of Eastern Orthodoxy (with its doctrine of the descent of the Holy Spirit upon the entire congregation) will give us some of the sources of this pattern of socialisation. No anti-Confucian campaign of rectification of thought in China will convince Sinologists that Maoism does not draw heavily upon Chinese tradition. The systematic onslaught on bureaucracy and hierarchy in Maoism may teach us how traditions are selectively interpreted by new generations in moments of historical discontinuity. It may also teach us how successful revolutions both start anew and reach back into the past. For nearly two generations, some of our colleagues in comparative studies have warned us that not simply our generalisations but our concepts would have to be revised, if a truly general sociology were to be developed. We have listened dutifully, but we appear not to have heard. Now, from within the historiography of the West, there is yet another shock. An historian of ideas, Blumenberg, has argued that the idea of secularisation (so central to sociological theory) is a residuum of the religious history of the West. If so, the implicit historical sequence assumed by much of our work will have to be revised – but how, and in which direction?

The large interest in structuralism of the past decades has important implications for us, despite the obvious impossibility of equating all of the structuralist ideas to one another, with respect to content, method or scope. Many of the structuralisms attribute a considerable autonomy to symbolic systems. In structuralist logic, this has consequences rather larger than the familiar empirical assertion that symbolic systems direct human action. Structuralist analyses deal precisely with the properties of symbolic systems in their interaction with other aspects of social process. They emphasise an order of constraint, not simply a type of random constraint. It follows that the relationship of social structure to cultural process can proceed only by an examination of the intrinsic organisation of culture.

The most obvious instance of this would be in linguistics. Historical linguistics has long been employed as a method of historical investigation. Structural linguistics presents different problems. Chomsky thinks language is evidence for an intrinsic human reason. His own radical politics are related to this position, since an intrinsically rational humanity can construct rational political community. Scepticism about Chomsky's Cartesianism cannot exclude large questions of the sort he asks. The structures of language are complex, efficacious and subtle – whilst ordered. Institutions cannot be characterised in the same way, far from it. Why is humanity capable of so much collective creativity in a language, and so desperately (even suicidally) impoverished in other spheres of existence?

The structural study of myth and art may answer more precise questions about society. The banishment to the symbolic sphere of disappointments and utopias may provide evidence of profound social conflicts, but it may also fix provisional solutions in an unintended permanence. Lévi-Strauss' claim to have established not a consonance but an identity in the structures of social exchange and communication enables us to examine hitherto obscure realms of human discourse. Suppose, however, that the laws of combination adumbrated by Lévi-Strauss are subject to purposeful modification? Let us recall this. When Marx developed his theory of alienation, of the fragmentation of human substance and the impossibility of human fulfillment, he recurred to Schiller's theory of aesthetics. Schiller argued that humanity was never more itself, indeed, only itself, in art. Aesthetic experience was distinctive because in it, the separated powers of a torn humanity were reunited. Most sociologies of art deal with the social conditions of aesthetic production. Suppose we were to ask, under what conditions can art become life? An inquiry into the possibilities of moving from art to existence would constitute an exercise in decoding of a kind ordinary structuralism hardly enjoins upon us. However, that may be asking a lot: we have hardly begun to appreciate the implications of the structuralist analysis of culture as it is.

The familiar idea of the objectification of the human spirit in the formal structures of culture raises, then, the question of the nature of that human spirit, the nature of human nature. The structuralist response is not all that different from a conventional sociological one. We never know the spirit, only its expressions – just as we cannot know a human nature apart from the institutions in which existence occurs. These are satisfactory formulations, with the difficulty that they ignore the legacy of Sigmund Freud. (It is worth remarking that Piaget, who thinks that structuralism as a method expresses a specifically human capacity to construct its world, is reasonably close to psychoanalysis.)

Classical psychoanalysis has a category termed 'defense by incorporation'. Sometimes, sociological theory has provided an instance of that process in its assimilation of psychoanalytic theory. The super-ego has been depicted as the repository of social norms, the ego as reconciling the conflicting claims of person and role. It would be gratuitous to deny the utility of these observations – but much more is at stake. Psychoanalysis constitutes a theoretical system, not a repository of descriptions of separate aspects of the psyche.

Two major theoretical efforts to integrate psychoanalysis with sociology may be instructive. The first was, and is, the examination of the relationship of Marxism to psychoanalysis. Much of this work was done in Europe in the 1920s and early 1930s; a recent revival of interest in Europe has taken up the discussion. The idea of a repressive society of course was consonant with the revolutionary aims of Marxism – but what were Marxists to make of Freud's belief that a large amount of instinctual renunciation was the price of the achievements of culture? There were other, no less fundamental, difficulties. The metahistorical core of Marxist theory is to be found in the idea of alienation and of the possibility of its transcendence. The analagous element in psychoanalysis is in the process of therapeutic recovery or self-recovery. Yet the recovered self is free – to live in a society characterised by the pervasiveness of alienation. The weight of Freud's metahistory, further – the struggle between Eros and Thanatos – entailed a cyclical and not a progressive interpretation of history. Marcuse and Mitchell have, each in very different ways, historicised our understanding of Freud. Marcuse, in the idea of surplus repression, has examined the consequences of a post-scarcity economy. In his view, it would eliminate the social Darwinism of Freud's social theory – and release the liberating potential of psychoanalysis, which would then work for human recovery in a world which could in fact be humanised. Mitchell, by contrast, insists on the extreme usefulness of the psychoanalytic depiction of child socialisation and psychosexual development in a society in which the patriarchal family is a residue of centuries of unequal economic relationships. The internalisation of these relationships in character development is not, in her view, an artefact of psychoanalytic theory: the theory, instead, deals with the actual content of history. Mitchell reminds us, additionally, that unconscious psychic function is the form of human existence. The value of both attempts at thinking about psychoanalysis is that historicisation, for these two thinkers, is not identical with an external sociologicisation: they do not reduce psychoanalysis to a sociology of the family, the better to dismiss unconscious psychic function as an unnecessary theoretic complication.

Neither Marcuse nor Mitchell are usually associated directly with the work of the psychohistorians, but the connection is there. Psychohistory is one of two things. It is an effort to apply psychoanalytic categories to historical data. More importantly, it is also an effort to revise those categories by combining them, theoretically, with historical inquiry – specifically with inquiry into historical change. The work of Erikson, Keniston, Lifton, Mitscherlich is psychohistorical in this second sense. It goes beyond, therefore, attempts to delineate and depict modal character structures in specific societies. (Academic memory in the social sciences is short: I am aware that contemporary psychohistorians had distinguished predecessors, Mead and Sapir amongst them.)

What would be the consequences for sociology of taking seriously Erikson's work on identity and his idea of pseudospeciation? The first is more than an application of psychoanalytic ego theory to social process: it identifies not merely objects but subjects of change. The internalisation of change, in other words, has to precede a new objectification: if institutions require personalities adapted to them, the converse applies. Erikson's view of humanity's creative capacity may exaggerate it and he may, as a psychoanalytic critique of his work would insist, join ego function to social necessity in a way that erodes analytical precision. He does, however, introduce an historical dimension into social thought where we might least expect it, in psychic function itself. His view of pseudo-speciation, further, rests on a theory of sociability which anticipates a global society. It is one of those meta-historical assumptions which calls much else into question. And, while sociologists study death, would they not do well to consider Lifton's assertion that the symbolic struggle against biological necessity is as important a component of psychic existence (if not more so) that the problem of sexuality?

Psychohistory places the psyche at the confluence of biology and history. We now learn from our colleagues in biology, ethology and physical anthropology that what we had thought of as biology, or nature, is subject to history. Humanity had no precise biological determinant: the process of humanisation affected biological evolution. I am at a loss to explore the implications of this change in our viewpoint, but the kind of work being done by our colleagues Morin and Moscovici has the promise of recasting many of our ideas of sociability. At the very least, it puts the contemporary ecological discussion in a more serious framework.

Finally, a glance at recent work in the philosophy of science will tell us that not the least of the reification in sociology can be found in the complacent belief that positivistic conceptions of the development and structure of science are still tenable. Kuhn's work on scientific paradigms is important, the work by himself and others on the sources of change in paradigms is more so. With the development of a school of critical science, natural science itself has become the object of the kind of reflective inquiry once dismissed in sociology as a residue of a metaphysical epoch.

One of the questions this raises for us is whether a strict demarcation between a philosophy of science and a sociology of science can be maintained. With his usual acumen, a gift for seizing upon questions whose time has come, Habermas has begun the exploration of the problem. Rather, he has continued it. A precise self-depiction, a sense of the historicity of thought has characterised much that still lives in the sociological tradition. The assertion of thought's historicity, however, carries with it the obligation to think and think again. A sociology which thinks only about itself, or confines itself to a world of its own objects, is certain to lose its capacity to make significant connection with the movement of thought. A sociology which seeks that connection may, however, question the necessity of its continuing existence.

IV. SOME TENTATIVE CONCLUSIONS

One of the least appealing aspects of contemporary sociology is its programmatic nature, its perennial announcement of developments to come. How much is written in the style of that application for a grant in aid of research which declares that, although at the moment, nothing is known about the problem – after the research, nothing more will need to be known about it! Statements about the direction sociology should take, even if in the form of serious attempts to confront our inner crisis, partake of this disorder, an advanced form of intellectual narcissism. I cannot in all honesty claim to have fully escaped the syndrome. The brevity, as well as the tentativeness, of these conclusions may show that I have at least begun to struggle against it.

It is clear that much of the work which the sociological tradition encompassed is being accomplished in fields other than sociology. That is a tribute to the strength of the tradition – even in the period of its decomposition. It is not invariably a tribute to ourselves. Meanwhile new structures of thought, new types of enquiry, deal with the phenomena of contemporary history peculiar to the post-bourgeois epoch. Finally, there are processes of intellectual development, accumulation and innovation: in the human sciences, most if not all of these are not to be found in sociology.

I have suggested that we look elsewhere for ideas, and given some indication of where we might find them. I have not been able to suggest how these ideas can be combined with many of our present concerns, for two reasons. One is that the project, if worthwhile, is intrinsically difficult and can only be proceeded with empirically – not programmatically. The other is that in many areas our intervention would be gratuitous: whole fields of the human sciences are doing perfectly well without us, and we are not needed. Certainly, nothing we can gain from other fields will restore our lost inner unity – more real, in any event, to recollection than in the actual past. The present situation of chaos within sociology, occasionally presented as a benign intellectual pluralism (who, precisely, is deceived by this?) will continue.

Sociologists are clearly unlikely to subscribe in their majority to a single method or doctrine. Marxists and structuralists, in any case, are found in a variety of fields. Sociologists are equally unlikely to accept that the temporality of social structures is their chief interest ; in that case they would seek certification as historians. Human nature, if too important to be left psychologists and psychoanalysts, is not the exclusive province of one field. The economists are doing badly, for the moment, but not so badly that they require our assistance. I could lengthen the list, but to what effect?

I would suggest a rather different course. Many of us are primarily interested in society and secondarily in sociology. The analysis of society presents problems, some of them very profound, none of them easy. Many of our contemporaries are doing interesting work on society, much of it quite unclassifiable in the conventional academic categories. Why not join them on the frontiers of thought, instead of persisting in the attempt to construct a solipsistic universe of discourse? Sociology may gradually lose its distinctiveness, as our efforts combine in a new science of society. That would hardly be a tragedy: the new science would continue that attempt at synthesis and contemporaneity which have given dignity to the sociological tradition. That, however, is a somewhat distant prospect. For the moment, the most effective way to be loyal to the tradition is to accept the consequences of its ending.

SELECTED BIBLIOGRAPHY

Abdel-Malek, A. *La dialectique sociale,* Paris: Le Seuil, 1972.

Adorno, T. et al. *The Authoritarian Personality.* New York: Norton, 1969, pb.

——— and Horkheimer, Max. *Dialektik der Aufklaerung,* New York: Social Studies Assn. Inc., 1944.

——— and ———. (Eng. trs.) *Dialectic of Enlightenment.* New York: Herder and Herder, 1972.

Alberoni, F. *Statu Nascenti.* Bologna: Il Mulino, 1968.

Altvater, E. et al. *Materialien zur Kritik der Burgerlichen Okonomie.* Netherlands: Rotdruck, 1973.

Amin, S. *L'accumulation à l'échelle mondiale.* Paris: Anthropos, 1970.

Apel, K.-A. et al. *Hermeneutik und Ideologiekritik.* Frankfurt: Suhrkamp, 1971.

Aries, P. *L'enfant et la vie familiale sous l'ancien régime.* Paris: Seuil, 1973.

——— (Eng. trs.) *Centuries of Childhood.* New York: Vintage, n.d., pb.

Arlow, J. and Brenner, C. *Psychoanalytic Concepts and the Structural Theory.* New York: International Universities Press, 1964.

Aron, R. *Dix-huit leçons sur la société industrielle.* Paris: Gallimard, 1962.

——— *18 Lectures on Industrial Society* (Eng. trs.). London: Weidenfeld, 1969.

Attali, J. *La parole et l'outil.* Paris: Presses Universitaires de France, 1975.

Auerbach, E. *Mimesis.* Bern: Francke, 1946.

——— (Eng. trs.) *Mimesis.* Princeton: Princeton Univ. Press, 1968, pb.

Badaloni, N. *Il Marxismo Italiano Degli Anni Sessanti.* Roma: Riuniti, 1971.

Bailyn, B. *Ideological Origins of the American Revolution.* Cambridge: Harvard Univ. Press, 1967, pb.

Baran, P. and Sweezy, P. *Monopoly Capital.* New York: Monthly Review Press, 1968, pb.

Barthes, R. *Le degré zéro de l'écriture/Eléments de sémiologie.* Paris: Mediations (Gonthier), 1965.

——— (Eng. trs.) *Writing Degree Zero/Elements of Semiology.* Boston: Beacon, 1970, pb.

Basaglia, F. *La Maggioranza Deviante.* Torino: Einaudi, 1971.

Bell, Daniel. *The Coming of Post-Industrial Society.* New York: Basic, 1973.

Bellah, Robert, *Beyond Belief: Essays on Religion in a Post-Traditional World.* New York: Harper, 1970.

Berger, Peter and Luckmann, Thomas. *Social Construction of Reality.* New York: Doubleday, 1966, pb.

Birnbaum, N. 'Beyond Marx in the Sociology of Religion? in *Beyond the Classics? Essays in the Scientific Study of Religion.* ed. by Charles Y. Glock and Phillip E. Hammond. New York: Harper and Row, 1973, pb., 3-70.

——— *The Crisis of Industrial Society.* New York: Oxford, 1970, pb.

——— 'Critical Theory and Psychohistory' in *Explorations in Psychohistory: The Wellfleet Papers.* ed. by R. Lifton and E. Olson. New

York: Simon and Schuster, 1974, pb., 182-213.
--- 'The Politics of the Future'. Forthcoming volume of essays by the Occident Express Group.
--- 'Students, Professors, and Philosopher Kings'. *Content and Context: Essays on College Education* (Report prepared for the Carnegie Commission on Higher Education). ed. by C. Kaysen. New York: McGraw-Hill, 1973, 401-490.
--- *Toward a Critical Sociology.* New York: Oxford, 1973, pb.
Bloom, H. *The Anxiety of Influence.* New York: Oxford, 1973.
Blumenberg, H. *Die Legitimitaet der Neuzeit.* Frankfurt: Suhrkamp, 1966.
Bon, F. and Burnier, M. *Les nouveaux intellectuels.* Paris: Cujas, 1962.
--- *Classe ouvrière et révolution.* Paris: Seuil, 1971.
Botta, F. *Sul Capitale Monopolistico.* Bari: De Donato, 1971.
Bottomore, T. *Sociology: A Guide to Problems and Literature.* New York: Vintage, 1972, 2nd ed., pb.
Bourdieu, P. and Passeron, J.-C. *La réproduction.* Paris: Munuit, 1971.
Boyers, R. and Orrill, M. *Laing and Anti-Psychiatry.* Harmondsworth: Penguin, 1972.
Braudel, F. *Civilisation matérielle et capitalisme.* Paris: Colin, 1967.
--- (Eng. trs.) *Capitalism and Material Life.* New York: Harper Torchbook, 1974, pb.
Braudillard, J. *Pour une critique de l'économie politique du signe.* Paris: Gallimard, 1972.
Braverman, Harry. *Labor and Monopoly Capital.* New York: Monthly Review, 1974.
Bronfenbrenner, U. *Two Worlds of Childhood: U.S. and U.S.S.R.* New York: Sage, 1970.
Brown, M. *The Economics of Imperialism* Baltimore: Penguin, 1974, pb.
Berque, J. *La dépossession du monde.* Paris: Seuil, 1964.
Chaunu, P. *La civilisation de l'Europe classique.* Paris: Arthaud, 1966.
--- *De l'histoire à la prospective* Paris: Laffent, 1975.
Chomsky, Noam. *Cartesian Linguistics.* New York: Harper, 1966.
--- *Problems of Knowledge and Freedom.* New York: Pantheon, 1971, pb.
Cixous, H. *Prénoms de personne.* Paris: Seuil, 1974.
Colefax, J. and Roach, J. *Radical Sociology.* New York: Basic, 1971.
Coser, L. *Functions of Social Conflict.* New York: Free Press, 1964.

——— *Masters of Sociological Thought.* New York: Harcourt, Brace, 1971.
Crozier, M. *La societé bloquée.* Paris: Seuil, 1971.

Dahmer, H. *Libido und Gesellschaft.* Frankfurt: Suhrkamp, 1973.
Dahrendorf, R. *Essays in the Theory of Society.* Stanford: Stanford Univ. Press, 1968.
Deleuze, G. et Guattari, F. *Capitalisme et Schizophrenie, l'anti-Cedipe.* Paris: Minuit, 1972.
Demerath, N. J. and Petersen, R. A. *System, Change and Conflict. A Reader on Contemporary Sociological Theory and the Debate Over Functionalism.* New York: Free Press, 1967.
Derrida, J. *La Dissemination.* Paris: Seuil, 1972.
Desroche, H. *Marxismes et Religions.* Paris: P.U.F., 1962.
——— *Sociologies religieuses.* Paris: Presses Universitaires de France, 1968.
——— (Eng. trs.) *Jacob and the Angel.* Amherst: U. Mass., 1973.
Dreitzel, H. 'On the Crisis of Culture in Industrial Societies'. Forthcoming volume of essays by the Occident Express Group.
——— ed. *Recent Sociology, 2, Patterns of Communicative Behavior.* New York: Macmillan, 1970, pb.
——— ed. *Recent Sociology, 4, Family, Marriage and the Struggle of the Sexes.* New York: Macmillan, 1972.
Dumont, L. *Homo Hierarchicus.* Paris: Gallimard, 1967.
——— (Eng. trs.) *Homo Hierarchicus.* Chicago: Univ. of Chicago, 1974.

Ecco, H. *Opera Aperta,* 2nd ed. Milan: Bompiani, 1967.
Emmanuel, A. *L'échange inégal.* Paris: Maspero, 1972.
——— (Eng. trs.) *Unequal Exchange.* New York: Monthly Review, 1973.
Engelsing, R. *Zur Sozialgeschichte deutscher Mittel – und Unterschichten.* Gottingen: Vandenhoeck, 1973.
Erikson, E. *Childhood and Society.* New York: Norton, 1951.

Farneti, P. ed. *Il Sistemo politico italiano.* Bologna: Mulino, 1973.
Fave, J.-P. *La critique du langage et son économie.* Paris: Gallimard, 1973.
——— *Theorie du récit.* Paris: Hermann, 1972.
De Felice, R. *Il Fascismo.* Bari: Laterza, 1970.
Ferrarotti, F. *Per una sociologia alternativa.* Bari: De Donato, 1972.
——— and Cipriani, R. *Sociologia del fenomeno religiosi.* Roma: Bulzoni, 1974.

Foucault, M. *L'Archaéologie de savoir.* Paris: Gallimard, 1969.
——— (Eng. trs.) *The Archaeology of Knowledge & The Discourse on Language.*
——— *Les mots et les choses.* Paris: Gallimard, 1966.
——— (Eng. trs.) *The Order of Things: An Archaeology of the Human Sciences.* New York: Vintage, 1973, pb.
Francastel, P. *La figure et le lieu.* Paris: Gallimard, 1967.
Friedrichs, R. *A Sociology of Sociology.* New York: Free Press, 1972, pb.
Fromm, E. and Maccoby, M. *Social Character in a Mexican Village.* Englewood Cliffs: Prentice, 1970.
Furet, F. et Richet, D. *La révolution française.* Paris: Fayard, 1973.
——— (Eng. trs.) *French Revolution.* New York: Macmillan, 1970.
Galbraith, J. *Economics and the Public Purpose.* Boston: Houghton, 1973, pb. (Bantam Books ed., 1975).
Gandillac, M. et al. *Entretiens sur les notions de genése et de structure.* Paris: Mouton, 1965.
Geertz, C. *The Interpretation of Cultures.* New York: Basic, 1973.
Gellner, E. *Contemporary Thought and Politics.* London: Routledge, 1974.
Genovese, E. *Roll, Jordan, Roll: The World the Slaves Made.* New York: Pantheon, 197 .
Giddens, Anthony. *The Class Structure of the Advanced Societies.* London: Hutchinson, 1973. (American ed.: Harper Torchbooks, 1975, pb.)
Ginzberg, E. and Solow, R. *The Great Society.* New York: Harper, Torchbook, 1974, pb.
Godelier, M. *Rationalité et irrationalité en économie.* Paris: Maspero, 1967.
——— (Eng. trs.) *Rationality and Irrationality in Economics.* New York: Monthly Review, 1975, pb.
Goldmann, L. *Le dieu caché.* Paris: Gallimard, 1955.
——— (Eng. trs.) *The Hidden God.* Boston: Humanities, 1964.
Gorz, A. 'Téchniques, téchniciens et lutte de classes'. *Les Temps Modernes.* Aug.-Sept., 1971.
Gouldner, A. *The Coming Crisis of Western Sociology.* New York: Basic, 1970. (pb.: Avon Books, 1971, New York).
Greenberg, C. *Art and Culture.* Boston: Beacon, 1961.
Gurvitch, G. *Les cadres sociaux de la connaissance.* Paris: Presses

Universitaires de France, 1966.
——— (Eng. trs.) *The Social Framework of Knowledge.* New York: Harper, 1972, pb.
——— *Determinismes sociaux et liberté humaine.* Paris: PUF, 1963.
——— *Dialectique et sociologie.* Paris: Flammarion, 1962.
——— *La vocation actuelle de la sociologie,* **I, II.** Paris: PUF, 1963.

Habermas, Juergen. *Erkenntnis und Interesse.* Frankfurt: Suhrkamp, 1968.
——— (Eng. trs.) *Knowledge and Human Interests.* Boston: Beacon, 1971, pb.
——— *Legitimationsproblem im Spaetkapitalismus.* Frankfurt: Suhrkamp, 1973.
——— (Eng. trs.) *Legitimation Crisis.* Boston: Beacon, 1975.
——— *Protestbewegung und Hochschulreform.* Frankfurt: Suhrkamp, 1969.
——— *Technik und Wissenschaft als 'Ideologie'.* Frankfurt: Suhrkamp, 1968.
——— (Eng. trs. of above two titles, partial) *Toward a Rational Society.* Boston: Beacon, 1971, pb.
——— *Theorie und Praxis.* 4th ed. Frankfurt: Suhrkamp, 1971.
——— (Eng. trs.) *Theory and Practice.* Boston: Beacon, 1974, pb.
——— and Luhmann, N. *Theorie der Gesellschaft oder Sozialtechnologie.* Frankfurt: Suhrkamp, 1971.
Hahn, E. *Historischer Materialismus und marxistische Sociologie.* Berlin: Dietz, 1968.
Hamilton, R. *Class and Politics in the U.S.* New York: Wiley, 1975.
Harrington, M. *Socialism.* New York: Saturday Review Press, 1972. (pb.: Bantam, 1975, New York).
Haug, W. *Kritik der Warenaesthetik.* Frankfurt: Suhrkamp, 1972.
Heilbroner, R. *An Inquiry into the Human Prospect.* New York: Norton, 1974, pb.
Hentig, H. von. *Die Wiederhestellung der Politik.* Stuttgart: Klett, 1973.
Hobsbawm, E. *Industry and Empire.* London: Smith, 1968.
——— *Labouring Men.* New York: Basic, 1965.
——— *Revolutionaries.* New York: Meridian, 1975, pb.
Holton, G. *Thematic Origins of Scientific Thought.* Cambridge: Harvard U. Press, 1973, pb.
Horkheimer, M. *Eclipse of Reason.* New York: Seabury, 1974, pb. (Orig. pub. 1947).

––– *Kritische Theorie,* **I, II.** Frankfurt: Fischer, 1968.
––– (Eng. trs., partial) *Critical Theory.* New York: Herder, 1972.

Jacob, F. *La logique du vivant.* Paris: Gallimard, 1970.
––– (Eng. trs.) *The Logic of Life: The History of Heredity.* New York: Pantheon, 1973.
Jameson, F. *Marxism and Form: 20th Century Dialectical Theories of Literature.* Princeton: Princeton Univ. Press, 1974, pb.
––– *The Prison-House of Language: A Critical Account of Structuralism and Russian Formalism.* Princeton: Princeton Univ. Press, 1972, pb.

Katznelson, I. and Kesselman, M. *The Politics of Power: A Critical Introduction to American Government.* New York: Harcourt, Brace, 1975, pb.
Kolakowski, L. *Chrétiens sans église.* Paris: Gallimard, 1969.
––– *Toward a Marxist Humanism.* (trs. from Polish) New York: Grove, 1968.
Kolko, J. *America and the Crisis of World Capitalism.* Boston: Beacon, 1974.
Kon, I. *Positivismus in der Soziologie.* Berlin: Dietz, 1967.
Kroeber, G. et al. *Wissenschaft und Forschung im Sozialismus.* Berlin: Akademie, 1974.
Kuhn, T. *The Structure of Scientific Revolutions.* Chicago: University of Chicago, 1962, 2d enlarged ed., pb.
Kung, H. *Christ Sein.* Muenchen: Piper, 1974.

Lacan, J. *Écrits I & II.* Paris: Seuil, 1966.
Lakatos, I. and Musgrave, A. (eds.) *Criticism and the Growth of Knowledge.* Cambridge: Cambridge University, 1970, pb.
Lafeber, W. *The New Empire: An Interpretation of American Expansion 1860-1898.* Ithaca: Cornell University, 1967, pb.
Lasch, C. *The Agony of the American Left.* New York: Knopf, 1969.
Leach, E. *Political Systems of Highland Burma.* Boston: Humanities, 1970.
Lefebvre, H. *La vie quotidienne dans le monde moderne.* Paris: Gallimard, 1968.
––– (Eng. trs.) *Everyday Life in the Modern World.* New York: Harper, 1972, pb.
––– *La production de l'espace.* Paris: Anthropos, 1974.
LeGoff, J. *La civilisation de l'occident médiéval.* Paris: Arthaud, 1965.

––– and Nora P. *Faire de l'histoire, I, II, III.* Paris: Gallimard, 1974.
Lévi-Strauss, C. *La pensée savauge.* Paris: Plon, 1962.
––– (Eng. trs.) *The Savage Mind.* Chicago: University of Chicago, 1970, pb.
Lichtheim, G. *Europe in the Twentieth Century.* New York: Praeger, 1972.
Lifton, R. *History and Human Survival.* New York: Vintage, 1970, pb.
––– and Olson, E. (eds.) *Explorations in Psychohistory: The Wellfleet Papers.* New York: Simon and Schuster, 1975, pb.
Lipset, S. and Riesman, D. *Education and Politics at Harvard.* (Report for the Carnegie Commission on Higher Education) New York: McGraw-Hill, 1975.
Lodi, M. *Il Paese Sbagliato.* Torino: Einaudi, 1970.
Lorenzer, A. *Die Wahrheit der psychoanalytischen Erkenntnis.* Frankfurt: Suhrkamp, 1974.
Lukacs, G. *Geschichte und Klassenbewusstsein.* Berlin, 1923. (Reissued Berlin: Luchterhand, 1968.)
––– (Eng. trs.) *History and Class Consciousness.* Boston: MIT Press, 1971, pb.
Luria, S. *Life: The Unfinished Experiment.* New York: Scribner's, 1973, pb.
Lynd, S. *Intellectual Origins of American Radicalism.* New York: Vintage, 1969.
Macciocchi, M. *Dopo La Revolutione Culturale.* Milan: Feltrinelli, 1971. (Eng. trans.: *Daily Life in Revolutionary China.* New York: Monthly Review, 1973.)
Mallet, S. *La nouvelle classe ouvrière.* Paris: Seuil, 1963.
Mandel, E. *Traité d'économie marxiste, I, II.* Paris: Julliard, 1962.
––– (Eng. trs.) Marxist Economic Theory, **I, II.** New York: Monthly Review, 1970, pb.
Mandrou, R. *De la culture populaire aux 17e et 18e siècles.* France: Stock, 1964.
Marcus, S. *Engels, Manchester and the Working Class.* New York: Vintage, 1975, pb.
Marcuse, H. *Counterrevolution and Revolt.* Boston: Beacon, 1972, pb.
––– *Eros and Civilization.* New York: Vintage, 1955, pb. (Reissued in Paperback, Boston: Beacon, 1974.)
––– *One-Dimensional Man.* Boston: Beacon, 1964, pb.
Markovic, M. *Dialektik der Praxis.* Frankfurt: Suhrkamp, 1968.

--- (Eng. trs.) *From Affluence to Praxis.* Ann Arbor: University of Michigan, 1974, pb.

Marquand, O. *Schwierigkeiten mit der Geschichtsphilosophie.* Frankfurt: Suhrkamp, 1973.

Marx, L. *The Machine in the Garden,* New York: Oxford University Press, 1964.

Mayer, H. *Zur deutschen Klassik und Romantik.* Pfullingen: Neske, 1963.

Merleau-Ponty, M. *Aventures de la dialectique.* Paris: Gallimard, 1955.

--- *Phénomenologie de la perception.* Paris: Gallimard, 1945.

--- (Eng. trs.) *Phenomenology of Perception.* London: Humanities, 1966.

--- *Structure du comportement.* Paris: P.U.F., 1953.

Michel, H. *Sprachlose Intelligenz.* Frankfurt: Suhrkamp, 1969.

Miliband, R. *The State in Capitalist Society.* London: Weidenfeld, 1969.

Mitchell, J. *Psychoanalysis and Feminism.* New York: Vintage, 1975.

--- *Women's Estate.* New York: Vintage, 1973

Mitscherlich, A. *Auf dem Weg zur vaterlosen Gesellschaft.* Munich: Piper, 1963.

--- (Eng. trs.) *Society Without the Father.* New York: Schocken, 1970.

Moltmann, J. *Theologie der Hoffnung.* Muenchen: Kaiser, 1966.

Moore, B. *Reflections on the Causes of Human Misery.* Boston: Beacon, 1972.

--- *Social Origins of Dictatorship and Democracy.* Boston: Beacon, 1966.

Morin, E. *Esprit du temps.* Paris: Grasset, 1962.

--- *Journal de Californie.* Paris: Seuil, 1970.

--- *Le paradigme perdu: La nature humaine.* Paris: Seuil, 1973.

--- et al. *l'Unité de l'homme.* Paris: Seuil, 1974.

Moscovici, S. *Essai sur l'histoire humaine de la nature.* Paris: Flammarion, 1968.

Naville, P. *Nouveau Leviathan,* **I, II, III**. Paris: Anthropos, 1970.

Nisbet, R. *The Sociological Tradition.* New York: Basic Books, 1967, pb.

O.E.C.D. *Science, Growth and Society: A New Perspective.* Paris, 1971.

Offe, C. *Leistungsprinzip u. industrielle Arbeit.* Frankfurt: Europae-

ische, 1970.
——— *Strukturprobleme des kapitalistischen Staates.* Frankfurt: Suhrkamp, 1972.
O'Neill, J. *Sociology as a Skin Trade.* New York: Harper, 1973, pb.
Ossowski, S. *Class Structure in the Social Consciousness.* (trs. from the Polish of *Struktura Klasowa W Spokecznej Swiadonosci.*). New York: Free, 1963.

Perroux, F. *Aliénation et société industrielle.* Paris: Gallimard, 1970.
——— *l'Économie du 20 siécle.* Paris: P.U.F., 1961.
Piaget, J. *Le structuralisme.* Paris: Uni. de France, 1968.
——— (Eng. trs.) *Structuralism.* New York: Harper, 1971, pb.
Poggioli, R. *Theory of the Avant-Garde.* New York: Harper, 1971, pb.
——— *Teoria dell'arte d'avanguardia.* Bologna: Mulino, 1962.
Poulantzas, N. *Pouvoir politique et classes sociales.* Paris: Maspero, 1967.
Preti, G. *Retorica e logica.* Torino: Einaudi, 1968.

Quaderni # 2; *Il Manifesto: Classe, Consigli, Partito.* Roma: Alfani, 1974.

Ravetz, J. *Scientific Knowledge and Its Social Problems.* New York: Oxford, 1973, pb.
Rawls, J. *A Theory of Justice.* Cambridge: Harvard University, 1971, pb.
Reich, W. *Sex-Pol: Essays 1929-1934.* New York: Random, 1972, pb.
Richta, R. *Civilization at the Crossroads.* White Plains: Int. Arts & Sci., 1971.
Rose, H. and S. *Science and Society.* Harmondsworth: Penguin, 1969, pb.
Rosenberg, H. *The De-definition of Art.* New York: Collier, 1973, pb.
Rossanda, R. *L'anno degli studenti;* Bari: Dedalo, 1968.
Rutkevich, M. et al. *Sociology and the Present Age.* Moscow: Soviet Sociological Association, 1974.
Rutkevich, M. et al. *Transformations of Social Structure in the USSR and Poland.* Inst. of Sociological Research of Soviet Academy of Sci., and Inst of Phil. and Soc., Polish Acad. of Sci., Moscow-Warsaw, 1974.

Sakharov, A. *Sakharov Speaks.* New York: Vintage, 1974, pb.
Salomon, J. *Science et politique.* Paris: Seuil, 1970.

Saussure, F. *Cours de linguistique générale.* Paris: Payot, 1968.
Schaff, A. *Marxism and the Human Individual.* New YORK: McGraw-Hill, 1970, pb., (Eng. trs. of the Polish: *Marksizm a jednostka ludzka,* 1965.)
Schoffer, N. *Le nouvel esprit artistique.* Paris: Denoel, 1970.
Schorske, C. 'Politics and Patricide in Freud's *Interpretation of Dreams', American Historical Review.* **78**, 2, April 1973, 328-347.
Sebag, L. *Marxisme et structuralisme.* Paris: Payot, 1964.
Segal, H. *Introduction to the Work of Melanie Klein.* London: Hogarth, 1973.
Sennett, R. *The Uses of Disorder: Personal Identity and City Life.* New York: Vintage, 1971, pb.
Shonfield, A. *Modern Capitalism: The Changing Balance of Public and Private Power.* New York: Oxford, 1965.
Soboul, A. *Mouvement populaire et gouvernement révolutionnaire en l'an II, 1793-1794.* Paris: Flammarion, 1973.
Steiner, H. *Soziale Strukturveraenderungen im modernen Kapitalismus.* Berlin: Dietz, 1967.
Stent, G. *Coming of the Golden Age.* Garden City: Natural History, 1969.
Stojanovic, S. *Kritik und Zukunft des Sozialismus.* Muenchen: Hanser, 1970.
——— (Eng. trs.) *Between Ideals and Reality.* New York: Oxford, 1973, pb.
Supek, R. and Bosnjak, B. (eds.) *Jugoslawien denkt anders.* Frankfurt: Europa, 1971.
Sylos-Labini, P. *Saggio sulle classi sociali.* Roma: Laterza, 1975.
Sztompka, P. *System and Function.* New York: Academic, 1974.

Tel Quel. *Théorie de l'ensemble.* Paris. Seuil, 1968.
Terracini, U. et al. *La Riforma dello Stato.* Roma: Riuniti,, 1968.
Thernstrom, S. *The Other Bostonians: Poverty and Progress in the American Metropolis.* Cambridge: Harvard University, 1973.
Thirion, A. *Révolutionnaires sans révolution.* Paris: Laffont, 1972.
Thompson, E. *The Making of the English Working Class.* London: Gollancz, 1965 (New York: Vintage, 1963, pb.))
Touraine, A. 'Crise ou mutation?' Forthcoming volume of essays by the Occident Express Group.
——— *The May Movement.* New York: Random, 1971. (Eng. trs. from the French: *Le Mouvement de mai ou le communisme utopique,*

1969.)
——— *Pour la sociologie.* Paris: Seuil, 1974.
——— *La production de la société.* Paris: Seuil, 1974.
——— *La société post-industrielle.* Paris: Denoel, 1969.
——— (Eng. trs.) *Post-Industrial Society.* New York: Random, 1971.
Trilling, L. *Sincerity and Authenticity.* Cambridge: Harvard University, 1974, pb.
Turner, V. *Ritual Process.* Chicago: Aldine, 1969.

Varagnac, A. *L'homme avant l'écriture.* Paris: Colin, 1968.
Verdiglione, A. (ed.) *Psychoanalyse et politique.* Paris: Seuil, 1974.

Wallerstein, I. *The Modern World System.* New York: Academic, 1974.
Wellmer, A. *Kritische Gesellschaftstheorie und Positivismus.* Frankfurt: Suhrkamp, 1969.
——— (Eng. trs.) *Critical Theory of Society.* New York: Seabury, 1974, pb.
Williams, R. *The Country and the City.* New York: Oxford, 1973.
Winkler, H. *Mittelstand, Demokratie, und Nationalsozialismus.* Cologne: Kiepenheuer, 1973.

Yankelovich, D. and Barrett, W. *Ego and Instinct.* New York: Vintage, 1970, pb.

Zambelli, P. *Richerche sulla cultura dell'Italia moderna.* Bari: Laterza, 1973.
Zdravomyslov, A. et al. *Man and His Work.* White Plains: Int. Arts & Sci., 1970.

NOTES ON CONTRIBUTORS

Norman Birnbaum is Professor of Sociology at Amherst College, Massachusetts, and Visiting Member of the Institute for Advanced Study at Princeton University. He holds a Ph.D. in Sociology from Harvard University, and has taught at Harvard, the London School of Economics, Oxford University, and the University of Strasbourg. Formerly President of the Committee on Sociology of Religion of the International Sociological Association, he was a Member of the Founding Editorial Board of *New Left Review,* and is an Editorial Consultant to *Partisan Review.* He is the author of *Crisis of Industrial Society* (Oxford University Press, New York, 1969) and *Toward a Critical Sociology* (Oxford University Press, New York, 1971).

Tom Bottomore is Professor of Sociology at the University of Sussex, and President of the International Sociological Association 1974-78. He was President of the British Sociological Association 1969-71. He is the author of *Sociology* (Allen & Unwin, 2nd edn. 1971), *Elites and Society* (Watts & Co. and Penguin Books, 1964), *Sociology as Social Criticism* (Allen & Unwin, 1975), *Marxist Sociology* (Macmillan, 1975), and other books. He is a contributor to *Encyclopaedia Britannica,Times Literary Supplement, New York Review of Books,* and other journals.

Amando de Miguel is Professor of Sociology at the University of Valencia in Spain. An alumnus of Columbia University, New York, he is the author of *Sociologia del Franquismo,*

Homo Sociologicus Hispanicus, Sexo, Mujer y Natalidad en Espana, and *Manual de Estructura Social de Espana* among other books.

Franco Ferrarotti is Professor of Sociology at the Instituto di Sociologia, Università di Roma, and editor of the journal *La Critica Sociologica.* He is the author of *Max Weber e il destino della ragione* (1965), *Sindicato, Industria e Società* (1967), *Una sociologia alternativa* (1972), and other books.

Ivan Kuvacić is a Professor at the University of Zagreb, and one of the chief editors of the magazine *Praxis.* He has written widely on philosophy of science, sociological theory, contemporary youth, and social conflicts, and has published *The Philosophy of G. E. Moore* (1961), *Marxism and Functionalism* (1970), *Affluence and Violence* (1970), and *Conflicts* (1972).

Igor S. Kon is Professor of Sociology and Senior Research Fellow of the Leningrad branch of the Institute of Philosophy, USSR Academy of Sciences. He is also Vice-President of the ISA Research Committee on the History of Sociology. He is the author of *Die Geschichtsphilosophie des 20 Jahrhunderts* in two volumes (*20th Century Philosophy of History* 1964), *Der Positivismus in der Soziologie,* 1968, *Soziologie der Persönlichkeit (Sociology of Personality* 1971), and other books and articles.

Stefan Nowak is Professor of the Methodology of Sociology at the Institute of Sociology of Warsaw University, Poland, and President of the Research Committee on Logic and Methodology of Sociology of the ISA. He holds a Ph.D. from the University of Warsaw, and has been a Visiting Professor at Columbia University, New York; University of Bergen, Norway; University of Lund, Sweden, Helsinki University, Finland; and Fellow at the Center for Advanced Study in the Behavioral Sciences, Stanford, California. He is the author of *Studies in the Methodology of the Social Sciences* (Warsaw, 1965), *Methodology of Sociological Investigations* (Warsaw, 1970), and has edited and contributed to *Methodological Problems of Sociological Theories* (Warsaw 1971) and *Theories of Attitudes* (Warsaw, 1973).

A. K. Saran is Professor of Sociology at Jodhpur University, India. He was formerly at Lucknow University, and at the Indian Institute of Advanced Studies, Simla, India. He has been Visiting Lecturer in World Religions at Harvard University, Kent Lecturer in Religion and Sociology at Smith College, USA, and Visiting Professor at California State University, Los Angeles, at Mt. Holyoke College, USA, and at El Colegio de Mexico, Mexico City. He has been a British Council Visitor to British universities, and contributed to the World Congress of Sociology held in Washington D.C., USA. He is a member of the board of editors of the journal *Ethics.*